Haunted Derbyshire

75p

By the same author:

DERBYSHIRE TRADITIONS

GHOSTS OF DERBYSHIRE

Of related interest:

GHOSTS OF THE LAKE COUNTIES

LANCASHIRE GHOSTS

YORKSHIRE GHOSTS

Haunted Derbyshire

by
Clarence Daniel

DALESMAN BOOKS
1975

The Dalesman Publishing Company Ltd.,
Clapham (via Lancaster), North Yorkshire.
First published 1975

ISBN: 0 85206 291 5

Printed by Galava Printing Company Limited,
Hallam Road, Nelson, Lancashire.

The ancient cross, now in Bakewell churchyard, beneath which Prince Arthur is said to have been forewarned of his death (page 32).

Contents

The front cover painting by Bruce Danz depicts the ghosts of a Cavalier and a Roundhead clashing swords in the Duel Room at Youlgreave Hall (page 69). The back cover motif is by Geraldine Rachel Hardy.

Photographs were supplied as follows:— J. Bricklebank, page 54; W. H. Brighouse, 33, 34, 53; P. D. Cooke, 36 (top); Derby Evening Telegraph, 55; E. H. Kyme, 35. Drawings are by the author.

Introduction

WHEN I wrote my earlier book on Derbyshire ghost stories, I tried to make it clear that I have no professional interest in the subject. Reactions to the book varied. One anonymous correspondent—obviously elderly and not very literate—was inclined to censure me by stating that he or she believed, as a Christian, that "ghosts were evil spirits". Another couple wrote, on the other hand, to thank me for strengthening and confirming their belief in the Christian faith. Another was grateful that I had not ridiculed or vilified belief in spiritualism. All of this was quite accidental and unintentional.

Interviewed on television, one questioner seemed surprised that I was able to reconcile belief (which I have never claimed nor yet disclaimed) in ghosts with the teaching of the Christian faith of which I am a lay minister. I had no hesitation in pointing out that John Wesley showed a keen interest in the supernatural and was at pains to record a number of experiences—including the disturbances suffered by his parents at Epworth Rectory—in his Journal. I also stressed that such prominent theologians as Dr. J. B. Phillips and the Rev. Leslie Weatherhead have testified in print their own experiences of seeing ghosts.

The Bible has a number of examples, including the reference in the 4th chapter of Job where we read that "a spirit passed before my face; the hair of my flesh stood up. It stood still, but I could not discern the form thereof: an image was before my eyes . . . ." Then we may recall that the risen Christ warned Mary in the garden, "Touch me not, for I am not yet ascended to My Father", and later the Beloved Doctor tells of the terror of the disciples who supposed they had seen a spirit. But on this occasion Jesus challenged them to touch Him—"Handle Me, and see, for a spirit hath not flesh and bones as ye see Me have". And as further proof He ate a piece of broiled fish.

But, again let me affirm that this is not a religio-scientific thesis. I am not trying to solve any mysteries, prove any theories, propagate any philosophy or proclaim any gospel. My researches have not been concerned with ouija-boards or playing cards, tables or tumblers, mediums, clairvoyants or seances. The book is just a collection of stories I have read or heard related and which have captured my casual interest, leaving me still without any psychic susceptibility or personal experience whereby I can subscribe to the countryman's creed and say with conviction —"I believe in ghosts".

1. The Frock-coated Phantom

WHEN they went to live at Over Haddon, the late Mr. and Mrs. Denham couldn't understand why such an attractive cottage in such an attractive village had stood vacant for three years. It was snugly situated upon the slopes of lovely Lathkil Dale, with charming views of the surrounding countryside. It was also convenient to Mr. Denham's place of employment at the D.P. Battery Works at Bakewell. And so they made the cottage comfortable and settled in. But it was not so easy to generate the atmosphere of comfort and cosiness the cottage had at first suggested, and it was then they began to realise why it had stood empty for the past three years.

Many times Mrs. Denham did not dare enter the pantry to make preparations for the evening meal when she was alone, for, although she saw nothing unusual, she sensed a malignant presence which induced in her a feeling of terror. She told me that no amount of money would have persuaded her to open the pantry door, and her state of tension was only eased by the return of her husband from work. She admitted never having seen anything herself, but affirmed that her husband and two nephews regularly saw an elderly gentleman with silk hat and frock-coat enter the gate of the terraced garden and walk along the stone-flagged path. The visitor was so real to the two boys that they sometimes amused themselves by shooting arrows in an attempt to dislodge his hat, and one Christmas they used orange-peel as ammunition for the same purpose.

The fact that she was the only one not privileged to "see" the visitor rather irritated Mrs. Denham, and she determined to at least "hear" him by loading the gate he was accustomed to enter with a collection of tin cans, the jangling of which would betray his approach. But, when he opened the gate to make his habitual entry, the cans remained silent! One evening when sitting alone in the parlour, Mrs. Denham heard a formal knock on the outer door, followed by the lifting of the latch and sounds of someone entering the room. Thinking that her husband had returned earlier than usual, she entered the outer room—only to find it empty. Looking out of the door, she was informed by a neighbour that a man had just left the house and walked down the road towards Lathkil Dale. But the sounds she had heard unmistakably indicated someone entering and not leaving the premises.

A local preacher with whom Mrs. Denham discussed these happenings suggested that the frock-coated gentleman may have died in unusual circumstances and that his body had never received Christian burial. He advised that upon his next appearance the burial service should be read over the restless spirit and this would terminate his wanderings.

*   *   *

Old Ned was a carrier who lived in the vicinity of Stoke Hall. A writer says: "There is a ghost story of a peculiar character about the ruins close by the River Derwent, and a few hundred yards from Stoke Hall. This old barn is said to be haunted by the ghost of Old Ned, a carrier, who hanged himself therein many years ago. It is said that he previously made many attempts on the trees around, but that the boughs gave way one after another, and that often at midnight he may be seen with a rope tearing off the branches from the trees, and finally disappearing over the crumbling walls into the ruins before mentioned."

*   *   *

A Wingerworth lady, proposing the vote of thanks at a W.I. meeting, told an interesting story concerning her employer when he was serving with the R.A.F. during the second World War. After a spell of active service, he was anxious to find some peaceful place where he might find rest and relaxation during the period of his leave. Driving into the country without any planned destination, he reached a secluded inn which promised to be a suitable retreat, and called to ask if accommodation was available. The landlord replied that he had a vacant room in which there were two beds, and put this at the service of the airman with the understanding that he would have no objection to sharing the room if the other bed was required. This was agreed and the visitor decided to retire shortly after the evening meal. Before settling off to sleep, he decided to read a book and was so engaged when he heard footsteps approaching his room. After a deferential knock, the door opened and a soldier entered the room and went over to the spare bed without entering into conversation with the reader. The soldier began to undress and prepare for bed, while the airman, putting aside his book, turned over and went to sleep.

When he awakened in the morning, the airman was more than a little surprised to find that the other bed was still vacant and showed no sign of having been disturbed by the previous night's sleeper. Then, adding to the mystery, it suddenly occurred to him that the soldier had been wearing the khaki uniform of the Great War and not the battle-dress of the present army. Upon going down to breakfast, the visitor mentioned the puzzling experience to his host who, instead of sharing his perplexity, quite casually commented, "Oh, you've obviously seen our ghost", and went on to explain that the soldier was a frequent visitor to that particular bedroom and was accepted as a regular guest.

*　　*　　*

Several people told me of an incident which happened a number of years ago and which was reported in a Sheffield newspaper. The story also appeared, much embroidered and altered in minor details, in the 1965 Christmas issue of a Matlock weekly newspaper. The story concerned a young courting couple who were riding a motor cycle combination one winter's night between Fox House Inn and Sheffield, when they were pulled up by a girl requesting a lift. She was dressed in a leather jacket and crash helmet, and gave a certain address in Sheffield as her destination. When they were approaching the outskirts of the city, the driver discovered that the girl—who had been riding pillion—was missing and decided to return as far as Fox House to try and locate her whereabouts. Finding no trace of the girl, he reported the matter to the police for their further investigation and resumed the journey to Sheffield. On second thoughts, the motor cyclist and his companion decided to call at the address given by the girl. The lady who answered the door was distressed by their enquiry, informing the callers that her daughter had been fatally involved in a motor-cycling accident and had been buried a few days before. And their description of the girl who had thumbed the lift matched the dead girl in every detail.

*　　*　　*

The December issue of **Derbyshire Life and Countryside** for 1964 contained two interesting stories of animal ghosts. A Derbyshire woman had moved house and, upon the first evening in her new home, was taking stock of her newly arranged furniture and belongings. While surveying the effects she felt something furry rubbing against her leg and stooped to stroke, as she supposed, her own cat which had accompanied her. But there was no cat to be seen! At that moment her own cat entered the room and reacted strangely by walking round and round—its fur fluffed up—as though appraising another animal in the centre. Then it spat and clawed at the invisible object before rushing out of the room, whereupon the mistress of the house heard a loud, contented purring, and again felt the sensation of a furry coat being brushed against her leg. The next day her own cat vacated the premises and never returned.

Calling at a Peakland inn one winter's evening, a visitor

10

found the bar deserted except for a black and white collie dog sitting by the fire. The man tried to coax the animal to him, but it ignored his attention. A farmer entered the room and the landlord proceeded to serve his two customers. When the visitor again turned his attention to the dog, he found that it had disappeared.

"That's funny," he commented, "I didn't see the dog go out. He isn't very friendly, is he?"

The other two exchanged glances and the farmer asked, "What dog?"

Upon hearing a description of the animal he hurriedly drank his beer and abruptly left the inn. The landlord explained that the farmer had gone to fetch his sheep from off the hills and bring them to lower pastures, for the appearance of the dog always presaged a heavy snowfall.

I have previously written about incidents when the Black Dog, or Barghast, has been seen noiselessly padding along on some sinister and mysterious mission, often disappearing into thin air before the gaze of the terrified observer. This was so in the case of two lead-miners at Bradwell who had been gambling with cards one Sunday and were stood in the Townend discussing their luck. It was a moonlit night, and one of them tried to draw the other's attention to a huge dog which soundlessly approached them and vanished upon reaching the place where they were standing. The other miner, unable to see the animal, scoffed at his companion's fears, but the latter nevertheless pleaded with him not to attend his work the following day as was his own intention. This advice was disregarded and the miner was the victim of a fatal accident, while the other became a thoroughly reformed character and henceforward led a religious life.

Mrs. M. A. Bellhouse, in **The Story of Combs—My Village,** tells of hauntings by a black dog at Cockyard:- "This dog appears from nowhere, at the top of the hill on the road to Combs, and walks behind one, right down the hill, when coming dusk. It makes no noise, acknowledges nobody, and vanishes into nothing at the bottom of the hill. I have experienced this and know it to be true. My Mother also saw it, when a girl. My husband, David, who lived at Rock Villa when a boy, reports that he and his brother panicked when they saw 'a small black dog' sitting on an island in the middle of floodwater near 'Michael's Cottage'. He and his brother both experienced the same fear, and 'ran like the clappers of Hell' for nigh on half a mile. Mrs. W. B. Jackson also experienced fear when she saw a black dog sitting on a corner of the Holderns, when she was a girl."

Mrs. Bellhouse also adds to the collection of stories concerning the renowned Dickey o' Tunstead, and has a reproduction of one of the many postcards showing the skull and telling of an offer of £100 refused for this strange talisman of good fortune. The skull was then in three pieces and had been re-assembled for the benefit of the photographer. She also records the interesting suggestion that the skull may have come from a prehistoric burial-place associated with Cadster Circle not far away, and also mentions that an Iron Age beehive quern was found at Tunstead Farm when drainage trenches were being excavated.

*   *   *

This chapter began with a story concerning Over Haddon and I am ending it with one which comes from the neighbouring village of Monyash. Several people—including a W.I. member —have told me that the wife of a former vicar had seen the figure of a clergyman standing in the church and always felt cheered and comforted as a result of these appearances. She was quite convinced that it was the spectre of a former vicar, the Rev. Robert Lomas, who came to an untimely end by falling over the Parson's Tor in Lathkil Dale when returning one dark night from Bakewell on horseback. Poems have been written on this local epic and for many years the tuft of grass found in his clenched fist was preserved in a glass jar in the church.

Tunstead Farm, home of Dickey's Skull.

Murder at the Miner's Arms?

THE Miners' Arms Inn at Eyam was built during the early 17th century, about twenty years before the village was desolated by bubonic plague, and during the intervening years it has generated that undefinable quality we call—for want of a better word—"atmosphere". Nor did a thorough restoration of the premises in latter years succeed in destroying that atmosphere, for it was carried out with sympathy and respect for its environment. This ancient inn was once the setting for the annual assemblies of the Great Barmote Court for the Joint Liberty of Stoney Middleton and Eyam—an arbitrary court of lead-miners entrusted with the responsibility of ratifying or revoking claims to possession of mines, settling disputes and administering the unique laws by which the industry was governed. The Court was authorised to establish rights of way to running water and the nearest highway, and to give miners permission to cut down timber for their underground workings. In the event of fatal accidents, the Barmaster acted as coroner and members of the Court (the Body of the Mine) as the jury. They also made and enforced laws which gave the industry virtual autonomy. The Court is still held in May, but the venue now is the village Mechanics' Institute, and it is still preceded by the simple refreshment of bread (formerly oatcake), cheese and beer served at the Bull's Head. After the adjournment of the Court there is a traditional dinner of roast beef and Christmas pudding followed by toasts drunk in punch and the smoking of clay pipes. Business meetings and annual dinners of the Eyam and Stoney Middleton Association for the Prosecution of Felons and other Offenders, founded in 1812 for the mutual protection of members' property and possessions, also used to be held at the Miners' Arms.

Once a bachelor clergyman and the landlord's daughter were the principal partners in a mock marriage staged in the inn parlour; a masquerade which caused such sensation and scandal that the bishop of the diocese decreed that the ceremony should be legally confirmed. Fun became fact, and this resulted in a breach of promise sequel with litigation costs which so impoverished the young clergyman and his wife that they had to take sanctuary in the village church to which a vestry was added for their accommodation. Their two children were born in church and they themselves spent their lives within its shelter, both being buried beneath its stone-flagged floor to prevent their bodies being seized in payment for debt.

Such premises, with such a past, could scarcely be anything else but haunted, and Mr. and Mrs. A. L. Hall—when living at the inn—stated that they heard footsteps proceeding along the bedroom corridor to the accompaniment of the rustle of a woman's dress. Their daughter, Wendy, then a girl of fourteen, felt conscious of an unseen intruder in her bedroom. She had a teddy bear for which she retained an affection into her 'teens, and this was sharing her bed at the time. Miss Hall felt that the presence was leaning over the bed, and clung for comfort to the cuddly toy until her feelings of terror and tension were relaxed by the assurance that she was alone again.

When Mr. and Mrs. P. D. Cooke took over the licence, they had only spent two nights on the premises when they had to retire to bed by candlelight due to a power failure. As they lay in bed they could hear loud, firm footsteps on the landing which should normally have been deadened by the soft pile of the carpet. The handle of one of the bedroom doors was seen to move and, upon searching the rooms with a candle, the landlord confessed that he had sensed "a definite presence". On another occasion, Mr. Cooke heard a clock being wound up in the small hours of the morning, while another time his daughter's record-player began to play when no-one was in the room. Again, he and another person distinctly heard a voice call his name —"Peter". The air on the landing was persistently cold, even when electric fires were switched on to warm the atmosphere, and electric light bulbs at the end of the landing were repeatedly fused. The phenomenon of footsteps used to be attended by a cupboard door being always found open—even after being carefully secured—in the morning, but this has been covered with hardboard and papered over to prevent the occurrence.

Mr. J. A. Carnall, chairman of Eyam Parish Council, reported having seen an elderly lady wearing elastic-sided boots, a black bonnet and a cape trimmed with jet sequins, enter the back door of the inn some time after its restoration. Mr. Carnall stated that she appeared to be confused and rather bewildered by the structural alterations. Both she and her attire belonged to an earlier generation and this was proved by her sudden evaporation. It has been claimed that over two hundred years ago, a landlord murdered his wife by pushing her downstairs, and it was wondered whether the heavy footsteps which defied the softening influence of the carpet and the rustle of skirts could have any connection with this happening.

*   *   *

Another Derbyshire inn which has memories of murder is the famous three-storied Newhaven Inn, a former coaching-house situated on the busy Ashbourne-Buxton road and built by a Duke of Devonshire. At the beginning of this century, J. B. Firth wrote that "it once provided stabling for a hundred horses, but most of the stalls have since been converted into cowsheds . . . . It now looks ghostly and deserted—save when the horse fairs are in full swing outside—but it used to have every bedroom occupied every night, and was as gay and fashionable as a London hotel. The Newhaven enjoys its licence irrespective of the whims of licensing magistrates, for George IV once spent a night there and was so pleased with his entertainment that he granted a free and perpetual licence of his own sovereign pleasure." The pattern of travel has changed insomuch that both stage-coaches and horse fairs would be a novelty, and the inn has adapted its services to cater for patrons of the petrol age.

Tradition tells of a violent brawl at this inn during a drinking session over 500 years ago. The struggle proved so fearsome that one of the participants died of fright and his body was dragged across the road and stakes driven through his heart to ensure that he was dead. Whether the victim of this barbaric act was interred nearby does not appear to be known, and, after all, it happened a long time ago. But, although bodies are disposable, spirits are not so easily laid to rest. The oldest part of the inn is reputed to be haunted: some people claim by the ghost of the murdered man. The ghost was described by Mr. George Hogarth as a "black and grey shadow which looks as if it hasn't got a head". He saw the apparition at the top of the stairs and stated that he went "cold—ice cold". Dogs have also shown a susceptibility to terror for no visible reason and one bolted upstairs to take refuge beneath the covers of its master's bed. On occasions when footsteps have been heard during the night, cellar doors which were securely locked and bolted the previous evening were found wide open.

*   *   *

At the Castle Hotel, almost within the shadow of Castleton Church, ghosts have appeared on several occasions. A broken-hearted bride was seen walking along the corridor to enter the raftered dining-room where, many years before, her wedding reception had been prepared and cancelled. All the arrangements had been made, but the bridegroom never arrived for the ceremony and the jilted girl died of an inconsolable grief. The maid who saw the white-gowned figure in wreath and veil ran screaming downstairs to tell her story. She was again seen by a more coherent witness who had observed that the figure was wading knee-deep in the floor-boards and was obviously walking on a lower and earlier floor-level. Another visitor was the Grey Lady, a small, elderly woman dressed in grey and with grey hair.

On another occasion the landlord and his wife, Mr. and Mrs. Philip Williams, were busy tidying up late one Hallowe'en night, when Mrs. Williams remarked that someone had walked past the frosted glass window into the tap-room. This seemed most improbable to Mr. Williams because all the doors were locked, but he went into the tap-room to reassure his wife, when, to his surprise, he saw the figure of a man with his hands behind him and standing with his back to the fireplace. His hair was turning grey and he was wearing a pin-striped blue suit. When Mr. Williams spoke to him, he simply vanished and the landlord returned to his wife with ashen face and his heart beating "like a drum". Another landlady had claimed to have met a man ascending the stairs and when she stood aside to let him pass, he also vanished. Few people had taken her story seriously, but she had always averred that the man was wearing a blue pin-striped suit!

Another public-house which is said to have a ghostly occupant is the Traveller's Rest at Brough, just opposite the Roman military station of Navio. This is the spectre of a woman dressed in black and carrying a bunch of keys. She was seen several times by Mrs. Dora Happs, a former landlady.

Another story told of the Traveller's Rest concerns a young farm girl who visited the inn one Christmas Eve, probably in search of fun and festivity as some relaxation from her duties in the dairy and on the farm. She was plagued by the amorous advances of a labourer who had been celebrating the festive season by over indulgence in liquor. His attentions became more and more insistent, so much so that the girl, in seeking to evade his sensuous clutches and suspecting his immoral motives, ran blindly from his presence and tumbled headlong down a spiral staircase to her death. Her spirit is claimed to return each Christmas Eve to haunt the place where she met her untimely end.

The 1974 Christmas Eve issue of Sheffield's newspaper **The Star** carried a photograph showing the present landlord, Mr. Con Sullivan, purporting to keep vigil with a flickering candle among the beer barrels in his cellar in the hope of catching a glimpse of the elusive spectre of the long dead girl. Mr. Sullivan admits to sensing a "presence" in the inn and stated that on one occasion he felt someone touch him on the shoulder, only to find, upon turning round, that the room was empty and the door closed. Another person, a customer at the inn, felt an unseen presence pass him on a further occasion.

3. The Witness of Some Well-known People

IN this chapter I intend to call some notable witnesses to give their testimony to the truth of psychic happenings, but would hasten to explain that the adjective "notable" is used in a local and limited sense and only as far as Derbyshire is concerned.

Writing over a century ago in his **Days in Derbyshire,** Dr. Spencer T. Hall tells the following story with all the sincerity of a man belonging to the respected profession of healing. It concerns an adopted girl living at Holloway, not far from Matlock and near the home of Florence Nightingale:- "Philip and his first wife, Martha, who was a cousin of mine, having no children of their own, adopted the little daughter of a young woman who went to live at Derby. The child called them father and mother as soon as she could speak, not remembering her own parents—not even her mother. While yet very young, she one day began to cry out that there was a young woman looking at her, and wanting to come to her; and according to her description of the person it must have been her mother. As no one else saw the apparition, Philip took her out of the house to that of a neighbour; but the apparition kept them company, talking by the way. They then went to another house, where it accompanied them still, and seemed as though it wanted to embrace the child; but at last **vanished in the direction of Derby** —as the little girl, now a young woman, describes it—**in a flash of fire.** Derby is about fourteen miles distant from Holloway, and as in those days there was neither railway nor telegraph, communication between them was much slower than at present. As soon, however, as it was possible for intelligence to come, the news arrived that the poor child's mother had been **burnt to death;** that it happened about the time when it saw the apparition; and, in short, that she was sorrowing and crying to be taken to the child during the whole time between being burnt and her expiration. This is no 'idle ghost story', but a simple matter of fact, to which not only Philip, but all his old neighbours can testify; and the young woman has not only related it more than once to me, but she told it in the same artless and earnest manner to my friend, the late Dr. Samuel Brown, of Edinburgh, who once called at the cottage with me."

*　　*　　*

William Howitt, the Derbyshire poet, vouched for the following story concerning his mother and uncle. The incident happened shortly after the poet's birth in 1795 at Heanor, at which time his mother's two brothers, Richard and Francis Tantum, both lived in the same parish. Francis was twenty years old at the time and was handsome, unattached, popular and a particular favourite of his married sister.

One sunny afternoon, while still recovering from her confinement, Mrs. Howitt was relaxing in her four-poster bed, the curtains of which were drawn to exclude draughts. She recognised her brother's footsteps coming up the stairs, heard him enter the room and saw him draw aside the bed curtains at the foot of the bed. He stood gazing at her with an unusually grave and pensive expression, until Mrs. Howitt asked him to come to the bedside so that she could speak with him, whereupon he closed the curtains, left the room and descended the stairs. Puzzled at this unusual behaviour, Mrs Howitt rang for her maid and requested the girl to recall her brother. The maid was equally puzzled, for she had neither seen nor heard the young man enter or leave the house. A search was made of every room and was extended to the garden and roadway, but still no sign could be found to explain his abrupt disappearance. At the same time a considerable commotion was heard in the distance, and there was the sound of shouting and excited voices approaching the house. Mrs. Howitt's enquiries as to the cause of the disturbance were evaded, but she became so agitated and emotionally upset that the news had to be broken that Francis had just been murdered.

It transpired that he had been travelling on horseback from Shipley Hall to Heanor and had called at the Rodney Inn for a drink without dismounting from his horse. The caller had jestingly flicked his whip at the landlord's son who had taken the order, and urged him to hurry, whereupon the youth rushed into the inn, snatched up a carving-knife from the table and returned to plunge it into the heart of the unsuspecting Francis. When the youth was tried at Derby Assizes, his counsel successfully pleaded provocation and the charge of murder was reduced to manslaughter for which a sentence of several months' imprisonment was passed. Upon his release from prison he returned to Heanor, taking over the inn at his mother's death and living a quiet and uneventful life.

*   *   *

During the early 1960s a Derby evening newspaper reported that the famous actress and cabaret star, Miss Diana Dors, had seen what was thought to be the ghost of a Jacobite wandering far from his native Highlands. She was staying at a lonely 400 years' old cottage at Swinscoe (just over the Staffordshire border) while playing in cabaret at the Dog and Partridge. She also took part in a special charity performance in aid of St. Monica's Church of England Home at nearby Ashbourne. On the Thursday night of her visit, she was suddenly awakened from sleep by the appearance of an apparition with long hair. Miss Dors confessed that she could not be certain whether it was a man or woman. "It certainly had long hair and was pretty horrible. I was scared."

Local legend recalls that when the demoralised troops of Bonnie Prince Charles were retreating from Derby in 1745, they passed through Swinscoe where several soldiers are said to have been captured and executed. It was thought that this historical circumstance might explain the mystery of the long-haired figure and that it was a Scotsman still haunting the scene of his humiliating defeat and death.

*   *   *

The late Nancy Price, C.B.E., a celebrated actress and author, related an experience she had when staying in a haunted house near Buxton during the early part of her stage career. She describes it at length in her autobiography **Into an Hour Glass.** The incident happened when, as a young actress, she was appearing at Buxton with the Benson Company. She and a friend considered themselves extremely fortunate in securing very reasonable accommodation at an old-fashioned house on the outskirts of the town. Neither gas nor electricity had been introduced into the house, and the bedrooms were illuminated by candles. The first night Miss Price sensed a malignant presence in her room; the second night she was awakened by a sensation as though someone or something was gripping her throat; while the third night she actually felt fingers tightening around her throat as a sinister voice whispered quite distinctly —"Remember!"

Although Miss Price had hitherto been perfectly well and strong, the strain of these three nights resulted in a breakdown of health, and she and her friend—who had occupied an adjoining room and helped each night to search the room for a possible intruder—decided to challenge the landlady concerning the happenings. To their surprise, the landlady, whom they had found a rather grim and forbidding type of person (perhaps because they belonged to a somewhat suspect profession), burst into tears and admitted that her house was believed to be haunted. She went on to explain that over a hundred years before, an absconding wife and her lover had been tracked down to that particular room and murdered by the jealous husband.

This story recalls a Christmas competition staged some years ago by the now defunct **News Chronicle** in which readers were invited to share their personal experiences of ghosts. One prize-winning contributor referred to an occasion when he had been cycling in the Peak District. Resting by the wayside at Wardlow Miers, he suddenly became aware of invisible hands gripping him by the throat and tightening almost to the point of strangulation. Recovering from this unnerving experience, he called in at the nearby Three Stags Head and there heard the story of the murder on New Year's Day, 1815, of the tollbar keeper, Hannah Oliver.

*   *   *

In his **Tales and Traditions of the Peak,** William Wood tells the story of a ghost in Eyam Dale which haunted the ruins of a cottage, the site of which is now occupied by a house enlarged from two houses built last century. Wood states that the figure of an elderly woman was often seen crossing the dell, and that the ghost assumed a variety of shapes and was sometimes responsible for stripping off the bedclothes while the terrified occupants lay trembling and frozen with fear. The figure was that of a "rather more than middle-aged woman wearing a short bedgown, linsey petticoat, mobbed cap and shoes with shining buckles."

The author tells how a tipsy lead-miner named Tom Loxley had an imagined encounter with the spectre after having repeatedly announced his lack of fear at such apparitions during a discussion on supernatural happenings at the nearby Golden Ball Inn. The woman with the mobbed cap and shining shoe buckles was prominent in the conversation. During the evening there had been much banter escaping Loxley's lips and much ale passing between them, and he was in a jocular mood when he left the warmth and comfort of the lamp-lit room of the inn to make somewhat unsteady progress up the Dale towards his home. As he proceeded along the moonlit way, tree shadows assumed fantastic shapes and the babble of the wayside brook suggested to the bemused miner that he was surrounded by ghostly voices engaged in an excited conversation of which he was the subject. Loxley's courage was now rapidly oozing away and he began to regret some of the rash statements he had made, especially as he neared the haunted cottage and imagined its ghostly tenant leaving the shadows and approaching him in angry confrontation. As his senses began to reel, the poor fellow staggered and fell to the ground whereupon icy fingers seized his ankles and dragged him relentlessly down the dell until he lost consciousness. Next morning the landlord of the Golden Ball found his previous night's customer lying by the side of the stream, his feet still immersed in the chilly water. This accounted for the icy fingers and helped somewhat to rationalise the events

20

of the previous night, but such was the effect upon Loxley that he henceforward lived a changed and sober life.

In the same book, Wood tells a story concerning a small mansion only a few hundred yards from the ruined cottage. This house is now the executive headquarters of a member company of an industrial group, and was once the home of Thomas Birds, an Eyam antiquary. It has entertained many distinguished guests including a former Duke of Kent, Joan Fry the tennis star, Lord Hill of radio fame, and other well-known personalities. The story concerned the year 1770 and was entitled **The Village Spectre.** Describing the contemporary house, Wood wrote:- "The delightful habitation of Mr. Weldon stood on the south-eastern verge of the beautiful village of E——; on each side of the mansion gardens sloped down to a great distance, in which were the choicest native plants and flowers. At one end of the dwelling rose a stately and thick-branched sycamore, beneath the shade of which Mr. Weldon would sit for hours every summer day . . . ."

Briefly, the story tells of a visit made by Weldon's daughter, Mary, to some friends in Lancashire where she made the acquaintance of the handsome Baldwin Laybrook, a young man of some social position, who promptly fell in love with the fair visitor. The affection proved mutual and, as a sequel, the impulsive Laybrook arrived at Eyam to request the hand of Miss Weldon in marriage. Notice of his intended visit had already been received by her parents in a letter of introduction, and he had planned to reach Eyam on the day previous to Miss Weldon's expected return. The same evening, after sitting beneath the sycamore tree with Mr. Weldon, Laybrook and his host were on the point of retiring to the house when they were startled by the appearance of "a shadowy form, seemingly clothed in a long white dress, which passed immediately in front of them three times in succession. It was the figure of a young female of elegant proportions; it had a striking expression of countenance, but deadly and cadaverous; still there was a calmness on that silent face which exceeded description; and on the colourless lips there 'loiter'd a smile, like moonlight on the snow'." Almost instantly the figure dissolved and a shocked Mr. Weldon exclaimed, "My God, the Spectre! the Village Spectre!"

This disquieting experience was related to Mrs. Weldon who shared her husband's sudden consternation and concern. After recovering some measure of composure, she explained to the bewildered visitor that the ghost he had seen was that of Isabel, the eighteen years' old daughter of Squire B——; the dash being a literary technique used with the obvious intention of implying the identity of a member of the wealthy family of Bradshaw, of Bradshaw Hall, Eyam. Isabel had been compelled to repudiate the affections of her true lover and marry a suitor chosen by her father. About an hour after the forced wedding ceremony, the reluctant bride received news that her despairing lover had taken his own life. She appeared to receive the tidings with indifferent calm, displaying no sign of emotion or grief until, a few hours later, she uttered a piercing shriek and died. And, concluded Mrs. Weldon, ever since the spirit of Isabel had appeared to foreshadow the "death of anyone whose heart the tender passion fills." The sequel to the story was that a messenger arrived shortly afterwards on horseback to break the news that, as the result of a false step, Mary had fallen from the coach in which she was travelling home and the vehicle had passed over her body causing fatal injuries. The accident happened about ten miles away from Eyam.

*　　*　　*

Wilhelmena Sterling, in her book **Life's Mosaic,** tells of an annual appearance in Bradwell Dale of no less a distinguished ghost than that of Queen Elizabeth I. It is said to commemorate the anniversary of an occasion when the Queen and her retinue, having lost their way to Haddon Hall, found temporary accommodation at nearby Hazlebadge Hall, another mansion belonging to the Vernons. This story is told on the authority of a family named Darneley which rented a summer cottage at Bradwell, and who were friendly with an old woman named Catherine. The latter lived with her brother and several cats in a low-roofed cottage in the village. Catherine was quite a character and was described as wearing her skirt "tucked high up over a red flannel petticoat, elastic-sided boots and a bodice with a kerchief folded inside the neck." The Darneleys were rather concerned that some of Catherine's tales might have a frightening effect on their young family, but the children themselves listened with fascination to her sinister stories. They were also eager to accompany the old woman when she visited the Dale to collect supplies of faggots for her cottage fire.

There was one particular evening in the year when Catherine declined to visit the Dale to gather her usual bundle of firewood, and was reluctant to offer any excuse or explanation to the curious children. At length, after much pressure and persuasion from 12 years' old Kathleen Darneley, she disclosed the reason for this departure from her accustomed routine, but made the girl promise not to divulge the secret to her parents. It was on this particular night that unsuspecting visitors to the Dale might see the ghostly cavalcade of richly caparisoned horses, with the regal figure of Elizabeth and her attendants. Catherine claimed that she herself had once seen this phantom royal procession, and that it was commonly believed that those upon whom the

Queen cast her imperious glance would be the victims of misfortune, but those who heard the tinkle of the harness bells would enjoy good fortune.

An old Bradwellian who knew Catherine Pearson and her brother, Larry, also remembered the Darneleys and the house where they lived. He described the Pearsons as simple old souls, and recalled that Larry was a person who never enjoyed continuous employment for physical reasons. When the Old Age Pension scheme was introduced, Larry became heir to princely riches by the weekly receipt of five shillings, making him henceforward independent of manual labour. He bargained to sell his wheelbarrow (the stock-in-trade of his working possessions) to a neighbour for ten shillings, but the latter made a counter-bid of nine shillings whereupon the barrow changed hands with alacrity.

Bradwell Dale has another story of the ghost of a jilted woman. Tilley tells the story in his **Old Halls and Manors of Derbyshire** as follows:- "On any wild night, says tradition, when the wind howls furiously and the rain falls in torrents, there can be seen in the gorge between Bradwell and Hazlebadge the spirit of a lady on horseback, the steed rushing madly in the direction of old Hazlebadge Hall. They say it is the ghost of Margaret Vernon, the last of the line of Vernons who were living at Hazlebadge for three centuries. She had given her heart, with all its fullness of affection, into the keeping of one who had plighted his troth with another, and when she discovered his treachery, she had braced up her nerves to witness his union in Hope Church; but at the finish of the ceremony she had ridden to her home as if pursued by fiends, with eyeballs starting from their sockets, and her brain seized with a fever, from which she would have never recovered, only for the tender nursing of those around her. Her spirit, they say, on a spectre steed, still rushes madly between Hope and Hazlebadge at midnight."

*　　*　　*

When I had spoken to members of Renishaw W.I. on my first "Ghost story" visit in 1962, I was urged to write to Lord Grey de Ruthyn, of Barlboro' House, with the assurance that he would be prepared to enlighten me as to whether, or not, his house was haunted, at the same time settling a mild argument evoked during question-time. Graciously acknowledging my subsequent enquiry, his Lordship wrote in reply: "Apart from a white lady (whom I have not seen) this house is quite free from ghosts. Barlboro' Hall has a white lady, too, I am told. I often hear noises in my bedroom at night, but don't pay any attention to them now. I did once see a wraith floating in the air in the churchyard. This was at 10-30 in double summer time."

23

4. Some Stories of the Stately Homes

And while we shared that sun-warmed seat,
Did she herself, in ghostly state,
Mount that same stair on silent feet
And pass invisible, the gate;
To stand in that neglected plot
Beside the fretted parapet,
And ponder, if the happier lot
Were to remember, or forget?

THESE fantasy lines were written by J. McCormack and concern the moat-encircled bower at Chatsworth, where the exiled Queen of Scots was allowed some measure of liberty for the purposes of exercise and relaxation while in the custody of the Sixth Earl of Shrewsbury. When her eyes grew tired, and she was weary of needle and embroidery, she was allowed to pace this stone-paved enclosure to while away the tedious hours of watching and waiting and hoping. And one wonders whether the ghosts of such outstanding personalities still haunt the places with which they were familiar in life. In this particular instance, we might well imagine the enduring impressions, etched upon her memory by the acid action of hate and revulsion, would be so bitter, and so powerful, that the discarnate sovereign would shrink from revisiting the place and reviving its unhappy memories.

Although there appear to be no records of ghosts at Chatsworth, the visitor would expect to hear some stories of spectres gliding along its corridors and up its staircases or across its lawns and through its gardens. So many famous people have lived there or enjoyed hospitality and entertainment within its walls. Many famous faces look down from gilded frames or gaze with unseeing eyes from marble pedestals, and one almost expects to see them suddenly regenerated in response to the resurrection fanfare of carved angels with uplifted trumpets. But no, they are as dead as the past to which they belong.

One of the former owners of Chatsworth, when Lord Hartington, gave a vivid account of having seen a ghostly monk at Bolton Abbey when on a shooting holiday with several distinguished guests including King George V. The incident happened on August 18th, 1912, when he was staying as guest at the Rectory. The ghost was looking past the Marquis and not at him, and it was standing at the door of his bedroom to which he was retiring at about 11-15 p.m. He immediately realised that it was a ghost, but felt no fear at the time. The figure "was below the middle height and seemed to be an old man of sixty-five or so. His face was unusually round, or, rather broad in proportion to its length, and was very heavily lined and wrinkled. The eyes were bright and the face might have been that of an old woman, but for the fact that there was about a week's growth of greyish stubble on the chin. There was a hood over the head and he was dressed in a long garment like a dressing-gown. The hood and shoulder seemed to be grey, but lower down the colour was black or brown . . . . There was no question of his being transparent; he was as solid as any actual man." The Rector had seen the same figure, and agreed that his face was very round and also that he looked as though he had not shaved for four or five days. Which provokes the question: Do ghosts shave?

*   *   *

An estate worker at Haddon Hall told me of a colleague who was convinced that he had seen the spectre of the renowned Dorothy Vernon lingering in the vicinity of her elopement. How fascinating it would have been if he had been able to report a re-enactment of that most romantic happening in the annals of Haddon! Another employee—while on fire-watching duties at the Hall during the second world war—heard strange and mysterious noises during his lonely vigil and attributed these to some ghostly intruder from the past. But the eeriness of the surroundings, combined with draughts and possible crepitation of ancient timber, and their effects upon the imagination, might well be calculated to induce mental impressions of phantom footsteps, creaking stairs and gently closing doors: on the other hand, the sounds may have been the genuine creation of some form of supernormal activity.

*   *   *

For a twentieth century housekeeper to receive a gracious vote of thanks from the lips of a seventeenth century mistress of the house must surely have been an impressive and unique experience. Yet this is claimed to have happened at Hardwick Hall, one of the magnificent mansions reared by the proud Elizabeth, Countess of Shrewsbury, and dedicated to her own glory. It was in the stately rooms of the south wing of the mansion—once the private apartments of the Countess herself—that she appeared to Mrs. Frances Stent, housekeeper at Hardwick for many years. Telling how that she had been awakened in her bedroom, Mrs. Stent affirmed:- "I saw the figure of Bess of Hardwick standing before me. She spoke kindly

25

to me and thanked me for looking after her house and its
contents so beautifully."

The room in which the grateful tribute was paid is reached
by a small staircase to the left of the great main staircase. And
it was in an empty corridor approaching this apartment that the
12 years' old Yorkshire terrier owned by a subsequent housekeeper often barked and whined excitedly, as though the instincts
of the animal were sensitive to some presence which was
invisible to human eyes and equally unrecognisable by the
other senses.

* * *

Barlborough Hall was once the home of a well-known Quaker
family; now it is the Roman Catholic College of St. Mary. Once
a great bow, reputed to have been that of Robin Hood, was
preserved at the Hall, and tradition makes the further claim
that this legendary hero was married to Maid Marian in a church
not far away. There is a story that the mansion is haunted by a
Grey Lady whose intended husband was killed in an accident
when travelling to church for their wedding. Each full moon
the melancholy bride is said to wander round the ramparts of the
mansion seeking the bridegroom who never reached the altar.
There is a "ghost room" where a recusant priest was said to
have been murdered while in concealment and it is alleged that
there is an indelible blood-stain on the floor.

* * *

Humid seal of soft affections,
Tenderest pledge of future bliss,
Dearest tie of young connections,
Love's first snowdrop, virgin kiss!

This well-known verse of Robert Burns is descriptive of the
warmth, passion and tenderness of a kiss. But, to feel the caress
upon one's lips of a cold, corpse-like kiss at midnight, must be
a blood-chilling experience. Yet this is the story told by Lord
Halifax in his **Ghost Book** concerning a famous Derbyshire
house—Renishaw Hall, home of the Sitwell family. When I
visited Renishaw W.I. for the second time to repeat my talk on
Derbyshire ghost stories, I was astonished to find that some of
the members had never heard this story which I introduced to
provide some variation from the stories told on my previous
visit.

During the year 1885, a large company of distinguished guests
had assembled at the Hall to attend the coming-out party of the
late Sir George Sitwell. Guests included the then Archbishop of

Canterbury, Dr. Tait, and it was one of his daughters who was the recipient of the macabre kiss. Miss Tait occupied a bedroom at the head of the staircase, and during the middle of the night she was roused from sleep by a sensation which she described as resembling three cold kisses. So vivid was the impression that she fled from her room and took refuge in an adjacent one occupied by Sir George's sister. Upon hearing the relation of this story, Miss Sitwell was reminded that she herself had once experienced a similar sensation when sleeping in the same room. Subsequent discussion and investigation revealed that others had known the same experience when sleeping in that room. Shortly after the party, Sir George mentioned Miss Tait's unnerving experience to his agent, Mr. Turnbull, rather expecting him to treat the story with ridicule, instead of which he turned very pale and replied: "Well, Sir George, you may make a joke about it, but when you lent us the house for our honeymoon, Miss Crane (sister of Walter Crane, the artist), a schoolfellow of my wife's, came to stay with us, and she had the same room and exactly the same experience."

The incident was temporarily forgotten until, at a later date, architectural alterations were contemplated at the Hall. These included altering and enlarging the staircase. Mr. F. I. Thomas, a cousin of Sir George, recommended that the haunted room and the one beneath should be demolished and incorporated into one staircase. While the work was being carried out, Sir George left instructions with his Steward and Clerk of Works that he should be acquainted of anything of note found during the process of alteration for both he and Mr. Thomas were interested in finding any evidence of the original plan of the house. Some while later, a letter was received by Mr. Thomas from the Clerk of Works urging him to come and investigate a strange discovery made during the removal of one of the floors. Upon arrival at the Hall he found that the workmen had uncovered an empty coffin fastened between the joists of the floor of the haunted room. The coffin was of antique appearance, having nails instead of screws, and was judged to be of 17th century date. It was securely attached to the joists by iron clamps and, owing to the shallowness of the space it occupied, had no lid—a component of funeral furniture which might have provided evidence of the identity of the original occupant. Although the mysterious coffin contained neither shroud, bones, nor other evidence of human remains, there were certain marks which suggested that it had contained a corpse.

One might imagine that the removal of the coffin and the virtual abolition of the haunted room would have been a sufficient means of exorcism to prevent the possibility of further weird manifestations, but not so, for on September 17th, 1909,

Sir George wrote to Lord Halifax to report further eerie happenings at the Hall:- "Last Saturday two ghosts were seen at Renishaw. Lady Ida had been to Scarborough to attend the Life Boat Ball, at which she had sat until four o'clock in the morning, returning home in the afternoon. After dinner, the party of six—I was absent for a few hours—sat in the drawing-room upstairs, Lady Ida lying on a sofa facing the open door. She had been speaking to a friend who was sitting on her left when she looked up and saw in the passage outside the figure of a woman, apparently a servant, with grey hair and a white cap, the upper part of her dress being blue and the skirt dark. Her arms were stretched out at full length and the hands were clasped. The figure moved with a very slow, furtive, gliding motion, as if wishing to escape notice, straight towards the head of the old staircase, which I removed twenty years ago. On reaching it she disappeared. Unwilling to think that there was anything supernatural in the appearance, Lady Ida called out, 'Who's that?' and then the name of the housekeeper. When no one answered she cried to those nearest the door, 'Run out and see who it is: run out at once.'

"Two people rushed out, but no one was to be seen, nor, when the others joined them and searched the hall and passage upstairs, could they find anyone resembling the woman described to them by Lady Ida. They had given up the search and were returning to the drawing-room, when one of the party, Miss R——, who was a little behind the others, exclaimed, 'I do believe that's the ghost!' No one else saw anything, but afterwards she described what she had seen. In the full light of the archway below, within twenty feet of her, and just where the door of the old ghost room used to stand, until I removed it and put the present staircase in its place, she saw the figure of a lady with dark hair and dress, apparently lost in painful thought and oblivious to everything about her. Her dress was fuller than is the modern fashion and the figure, though opaque, cast no shadow. It moved with a curious gliding motion into the darkness and melted away at the spot within a yard of the place where a doorway, now walled up, led from the staircase to the hall. There is no doubt that these figures were actually seen as described. They were not ghosts but phantasms, reversed impressions of something seen in the past, and now projected from an overtired and excited brain. In both cases the curious gliding motion, the absence of shadow and the absolute stillness of the figures, which moved neither hand nor head and hardly seemed to breathe, point to that conclusion. Such an experience goes far towards solving the ghost problem." Then Sir George concluded his theory with the rather contradictory statement: "Ghosts are sometimes met with, but they are not ghosts."

Tapton House, near Chesterfield, former home of George Stephenson who was heard to enquire why his water had not been brought to his room.

A note supplied by Lady Ida states: "I saw the figure with such distinctness that I had no doubt at all that I was looking at a real person, while, at the same time, although seated in a well-lighted room and chatting with friends, I was conscious of an uneasy, creeping feeling. I tried to see the features, but could not. Even before I called out, my friends noticed that I appeared to be following something with my eyes. The light in the passage was good and I could see so well that I could distinguish the exact shade of dress. The figure was that of a woman between fifty and sixty years of age and her grey hair was done up into a 'bun', under an old-fashioned cap. I have never seen a ghost, nor had I been thinking about ghosts."

*   *   *

Tapton House, Chesterfield, once qualified as a stately home. It was the residence of George Stephenson after he had retired from active participation in the railway, coal, iron and lime industries. The mansion had fallen into a state of dilapidation, but Stephenson applied his energies and money to its renovation and quickly transformed both the house and its environment. Here the renowned inventor devoted his leisure to pet dogs, rabbits and birds, as well as developing his interest in botany by growing tropical fruits and making such eccentric experiments as growing straight cucumbers in specially made tubes of glass. The house was later used as a boarding school, then became the home of the Markham family and is once again serving the present generation as a centre of education.

Some years ago, while the house has been performing its present function as a school, the caretaker's wife was busy sweeping a corridor on the first floor, at the end of which stone steps lead to a door which was locked at the time. While thus engaged, she was surprised to hear a masculine voice reproaching her with the words: "You didn't bring my water up today!" She found that the gentleman charging her with this neglect was a total stranger and noted with some curiosity that his style of clothing was that belonging to a former decade. In all other respects he was quite normal in appearance. When the complaint was repeated, the lady expressed a rather bewildered apology and went off down the corridor where she was met by her husband to whom she related her strange story. They returned together to the scene of the encounter, but the stranger was no longer to be found. Nor could he have made his exit by any other means than the door at the bottom of the steps which, the caretaker confirmed, was still locked. The incident was brought to the attention of the head of the school who produced an album of pictures and asked the lady if any of the portraits resembled the person she had seen. As a result of this identification parade from the past, she unhesitatingly singled out a particular portrait, declaring that he was the person.

"Do you know who that is?" asked the headmaster.

"No", was the innocent reply.

"That is George Stephenson."

•   •   •

Another hall which has changed in character and has been deprived of its former dignity and architectural status is Wheston Hall near Tideswell. I remember it as a much larger building than it is now and one which was occupied by more than one family. Structural alterations have been carried out to make it more compatible with modern domestic needs. In its heyday the Hall was occupied by the influential John Shaw, Steward of the High Peak Courts. The building used to impress me as being rather gloomy and cheerless, but that may have been the result of reading J. C. Tilley's **Old Halls and Manors of Derbyshire.** I have also recorded previous ghost stories related to me by a former resident at the Hall.

Tilley tells of a spectral spouse making an annual pilgrimage from Tideswell to her husband's unconsecrated grave at

Wheston. Usually, according to ghost-lore, it is the troubled spirit of the occupant of the unconsecrated grave who cannot settle in such an environment and seeks the amelioration of such a situation by human intervention to terminate its restless wanderings. But this was the reverse. Whether the woman was tortured by a vindictive conscience, or whether she was seeking reconciliation with her wronged husband, or whether it was in payment of a perpetual penance, no-one seems to know. But the debt now appears to have been liquidated and in recent years no-one appears to have heard or seen the anguished and unhappy ghost as "she passes three times round the house, barefooted, in her night-gown, shrieking and tearing her golden hair."

Tilley explains that this lady, in her lifetime, had been compelled to renounce the suitor of her choice and marry a man whom she loathed and detested, and to whom she could offer no pledge of affection. After this unhappy marriage, the rejected lover had retired to the seclusion of Wheston Hall where he had sought healing for his broken heart in the study of literature and the occult sciences. Villagers hinted that he dealt in the black arts and that his visitors had tails and cloven hoofs! But one day he had another visitor—the lady to whom he had given his heart. Finding her marriage intolerable, she had deserted her husband and fled to Wheston to become (it was rumoured) the mistress of her former lover. Then came another visitor to the Hall; the husband in search of his absconded wife. But this caller was never seen to leave by the vigilant village gossips, and beneath the fruit trees in the orchard appeared a sinister patch of freshly disturbed earth! At least, so the rustic observers reported. Time passed by. The two remaining characters in this rural drama died, and the lady was buried at Tideswell from whence she annually deserted the dark dominion of the tomb to make her sad pilgrimage to the scene of her husband's grave in the orchard of Wheston Hall.

A lady who had lived for many years at the Hall told me the story of "Soldier Dick"—the warrior who stood a solitary sentry in the reception hall, and whose removal caused disruption in the household or on the farm, but who, treated with due respect, protected the interests of occupants, house and farm. She also stated that there was a bloodstain on the cellar steps which resisted every attempt at removal by the application of soap, water and scrubbing-brush.

*　　*　　*

The story is told of a prince who once had a strange premonition of death while on a visit to Derbyshire. It is recorded that "Sir Henry Vernon was governor and treasurer to

Prince Arthur, elder son and heir apparent to Henry VII, and that the prince frequently stayed at Haddon where there is an apartment called the Prince's Chamber, with his armorial bearings cut in several places." Prince Arthur was a close friend of Sir Henry's son, George, who later became renowned for his sovereign acts as the "King of the Peak". At the age of twelve, the young prince had been betrothed in marriage to Catherine, fourth daughter of Ferdinand, King of Castile and Aragon, the ceremony having been performed in the chapel of the Manor of Bewdley.

During the September of 1501, Prince Arthur was guest of Sir Henry Vernon at Haddon Hall for the last time. As was usual during his visits to Derbyshire, Arthur spent considerable time exploring the district around Haddon, rambling in solitude among the woods and fields, and finding relaxation in the peace of the countryside. One evening he had wandered along the banks of the River Wye in the direction of Bakewell, and eventually reached the cross-roads at Hassop where stood the ancient stone cross which may now be seen in front of the Vernon Chapel in Bakewell churchyard. Deciding to rest at this spot, the royal youth sat pensively for some while on a grassy slope at the foot of the cross. As he lingered in deep meditation, he became aware of a "tall thin female dressed in white; her features sunken and wan, her lips of an ashy hue, and her eyeballs protruding, bright and motionless". Pointing her finger at the prince, she is said to have made the following prophetic utterance:- "Unhappy, royal Prince, mourn not that fate which is not thine! One earthly pageant awaits thee, yea, it is at hand; and then, ah! then, thou wilt drop into the lap of thy mother —thy mother earth! Forth comes to Britain's shore thy lovely, smiling bride—ah! bride and widow of a royal boy!"

When he rose to his feet, the perplexed prince found that his spectral visitor had vanished and he was all alone. Retracing his steps to Haddon, he was haunted at every step by misgivings and grim forebodings of ill as he brooded over the meaning of the mysterious message. When he neared the grey walls of the Hall he was met by his host and a party of servants who had been searching for him, and was greeted with the news that an urgent message had been received, requesting his immediate return to London. As foretold by the phantom, his Spanish bride had arrived and their marriage was to be confirmed without delay. The ceremony was marked with great pageantry and national rejoicing, following which the royal couple took up their residence at Ludlow Castle in Shropshire. Shortly afterwards the prince was taken ill, and, only four months after her wedding, Catherine was a widow. And the last words of her young husband had been "O, the vision of the cross at Haddon!"

Over Haddon church. At a cottage near this church, a frock-coated phantom was in the habit of entering the garden gate to visit the premises (page 8).

Above:— Barlborough Hall, said to be haunted by a Grey Lady
(page 26).

Opposite: Top: Hardwick Hall, built by Bess of Hardwick, Countess of
Shrewsbury. The Countess is said to have appeared and thanked a
former house-keeper for the way in which she maintained the mansion
(page 26).

Bottom: Queen Mary's Bower in Chatsworth House Park, a relic of the
ancient house in which Mary Queen of Scots was confined and where she
is said to have been allowed exercise (page 24).

The Miners' Arms, Eyam, where heavy footsteps were heard on a heavily carpeted corridor (page 14).

A post-card of Dickey's Skull (page 12).

5. A Chapter About Children

MANY children live in their own world of innocent curiosity and make-believe, and perhaps this is one reason why they are sometimes more sensitive to the supernatural than adults. They seem to have powers of penetrating the unseen which have been denied to some of their elders, and it would be wrong to write off the things they see and feel and hear as being just the products of their naturally inventive imagination. They have not cultivated that air of scepticism and hostility which many older people forge into a psychological armour to resist belief in things that cannot be rationalised or explained or understood. Such people live in a fortress of fear; a doubting castle; and in their superior knowledge and wisdom, feel it a duty to discourage juvenile belief in the miracles and mysteries of the supernatural. Personally, while I would strongly counsel children from cultivating a curiosity concerning black magic and its associated evils (a sphere which, admittedly, I have no wish to investigate), I still feel that they may have a special susceptibility to the supernatural because of the many stories which I have heard or read from time to time.

The following is a classic example from county history and was attested by Samuel Hutton, brother of William Hutton, the historian, and concerns a personal experience which happened in 1740: "At seven years of age I was set to work in the silk mills (at Derby), where I toiled from five o'clock in the morning till seven at night for the weekly sum of one shilling. This paid for my board and lodging, and rendered me independent of my father, except for the clothes I wore. There a remarkable circumstance occurred to me. Afraid of being past my hour in the morning, and deceived by a clouded moon, I frequently rose in the night, mistaking it for day. At one of these times, I found all was silent at the mill, and I knew that I was too early. As I stood leaning pensively on the parapet of the bridge, I heard a clattering of horses' feet; and, without turning my head, I asked what it was o'clock. No answer being given, I turned to look, and distinctly saw the appearance of a man, riding on one horse and leading another, on the mill-wheel. The clock then struck four, and the apparition vanished. The reality of this has been doubted. It has been urged that the intellects of a sleepy boy at such an hour were not sufficiently clear to decide upon so important a point as the appearance of ghosts. In short, that I must have been asleep; that the man and horses moving on the mill-wheel must have been the subjects of my dream, and that

I was awakened by the striking of the clock. But I am as certain that I saw them there, as that I have been relating that circumstance. I am not afraid of ghosts. On the contrary, the certainty of having seen one has made me desirous of meeting with others, and I have sought them at midnight in churchyards, and on fields of unburied dead. But I am as little visionary as I am afraid, and I own that I never saw any other apparition than that upon the mill-wheel."

* * *

In another chapter, **The Witness of Well-known People**, Dr. S. T. Hall tells of the experience of a small girl who saw the ghost of her mother. Gail Sharpe, of Eckington, was nearly twelve years old when she saw a ghostly female in an old cottage at Curbar where she was staying with her grandmother. The incident happened on the 10th June, 1970, and three years later Gail was able to describe quite lucidly what she saw on the morning of that day. Gail's grandmother was employed in the village as housekeeper at the time and had left her granddaughter in bed. Suddenly the girl was awakened by the sound of a voice which she thought was that of her Uncle Chris who lived at Chesterfield, and, sitting up, saw not her uncle but an elderly lady sat at the foot of her bed. The stranger wore steel-rimmed spectacles and her "grey hair was parted down the middle and screwed up into a bun at the back". She was wearing what the girl at first mistook for a black "poncho" (a South American type garment popular with children at the time), but which she later realised was a knitted shawl. This was around her shoulders and above what Gail rather vaguely described as a "black sort of dress". She also wore "a smile and looked very pleasant". Gail buried her head beneath the bedclothes until she felt calm enough to venture a further peep, whereupon she found that the visitor had vanished. She then hurried downstairs and fled in a distressed state to find her grandmother.

Both Gail and her grandmother were convinced that there was something eerie about the cottage. Footsteps were often heard crossing the landing and passing through the bedroom. Gail claimed that there was a "whirlwind" in the warmest room of the cottage and a feeling of chill in most of its rooms. Mr. George Goddard, a former Parish Council chairman and churchwarden for many years, was informed of the happening and on hearing the description immediately identified the woman as a former occupant of the cottage.

* * *

One family at Great Longstone named their house the "Little Church Lady House" because of a friendly wraith often seen by the children, yet remaining invisible to their parents. While sitting at meals, the children would quite casually draw attention to the fact that they had seen the "little church lady" going to wash her hands in a corner of the adjacent room. The name derived from the fact that the lady was always dressed in a sober black attire.

*   *   *

Although Mr. Francis Fisher, a former secretary of the Derbyshire Archaeological Society, is usually occupied with less abstract features of history and folk-lore than ghosts, he is never too busy to jot down stories of phantoms and haunted houses. With his permission, I pass on the following incidents he has recorded concerning Alvaston—a former village which is now absorbed as a suburb of Derby: "Still remembered is the strange story of the man returning home one evening who saw an aged woman walking unsteadily with a crutch. He followed her a little way to ensure that she did not fall, and watched her turn up the path to the village sweet shop. Before she reached the door she vanished! Recounting his experience later, the man was told that he had described to the smallest detail the appearance of the former occupier of the shop who had died some years before. The story was given publicity at the time—this happened about 1937—and the account seems sober enough.

"From a lady still living I have heard perhaps the most peculiar of all these stories. It happened to her and another girl with whom she was playing in Alvaston schoolyard. This would be about 1890, I suppose. From along the lane which led to Alvaston they heard the sounds of galloping horses, and indistinct cries. The report of a pistol and the approaching noise made them beat a retreat to safety at the other end of the playground. The horses' hooves sounded more clearly, came suddenly with a roar, and travelled past the yard. But there was nothing to be seen! A minute later came another clash of hooves, again to pass along the lane towards Derby. It was a frightening experience for two small girls, and one they never forgot. We know that there was a vigorous skirmish at Alvaston in the Civil War when Sir John Gell stormed the home of the Blounts and his guns peppered the church. Was this queer commotion something which was heard three hundred years ago, with eager Roundheads in hot pursuit of hapless Cavaliers?"

Mr. Fisher tells another eerie tale: "In the room above, a former occupant of the house had hanged himself. The tragedy was discovered when someone went to see what was causing the bumps on the ceiling. The dead man's heels were just touching the floor, and the wind was swaying the suspended corpse when the door was opened. It was a strange tale, I thought, for a

39

woman to tell her six-year-old nephew, but he had no terror of it, either then or in later years when he visited his aunt and sat by the fireside, listening to the bumps which would occasionally be heard on the ceiling above. The house was old, and bumps seemed natural; not so natural perhaps as the violent shaking of the heavy door at times which seemed as if someone outside was trying to wrest it from its hinges, but that again was accepted as common enough."

*　　*　　*

Ghosts of children are by no means uncommon. In **Ghosts of Derbyshire** I have previously written of the figure of a headless child seen simultaneously by four occupants of a car at Handley, near Clay Cross, and also of a small girl seen at a Chesterfield house now converted into bank premises. Meeting this particular child, a lady stooped to gather the little stranger into her arms, only to find that the figure had no physical reality.

During May, 1973, three demolition workers saw the ghost of a boy while they were working on the site of William and Glyn's Bank in the Corn Market at Derby. The **Derby Evening Telegraph** reported the incident and published a photograph by way of illustration. This showed an underground brick cavity supported by an iron girder. This had been discovered during the excavations and appeared to have been sealed up at some previous period. Had it contained human remains, this might have provided an explanation for the ghostly occupant, but it appeared to be quite innocent of any sinister circumstances. Mr. Arthur Holt, district manager of the bank, told the story of what had happened. "The men were apparently testing part of the foundations below ground level and knocked a hole through one of the walls to reveal a cavity which had no other exit. The figure of a small boy was seen in the cavity by all three men. They asked what he was doing there and received the reply, 'I live here'. He then vanished into thin air."

This story is one of the many which seem to suggest an element of timelessness, in which the past appears to be in contact and communication with the present. The boy from the past had the faculty to discuss and answer a question posed by persons in the present. At other times, to the contrary, a ghost seems to be in a state of complete abstraction and shows no hint of recognition when confronted by some person in the present. Perhaps some spirits have the gift of clairvoyance in reverse, while others —like many humans—are devoid of any psychic gift to cross the bridge between the past and the present.

*　　*　　*

Mr J. Willis told me of an occasion when he heard a child's greeting on three different occasions. He was employed on night shift duties at Litton Mills where textured yarns were then being produced. In former times this mill had a sinister reputation because of the harsh conditions under which pauper children were employed as apprentices. The horrors and hardships of these unwanted children were recorded from the recollections of one of their number, a certain Samuel Blincoe who described the long hours, poor meals, bad living conditions and sadistic treatment endured by the orphans and outcasts. Mr. Willis said he heard the voice quite distinctly in the stillness of the night and, although there was no other human present, he was convinced of its reality and that it was the voice of a child. It just said "Hello!" Mr. Willis looked round for the source of the sound, but he was physically alone. He heard the same word uttered on a further occasion and the third time, not being startled or alarmed, he responded to the greeting with a friendly echo "Hello!" Perhaps it was a wistful voice from the past of one of the pauper apprentices yearning for the comfort and companionship of which he had known so little in his lifetime.

Another worker in the cotton industry assured me that he had seen the shadowy figure of what he believed to be Sir Richard Arkwright, the cotton magnate, in the original part of the much enlarged Masson Mills at Matlock Bath. He saw the figure through the glass panel of a door in a part of the mill that was little used and was quite convinced that it was none other than Sir Richard. Nor was he the only person who had sensed or seen the same presence.

*　　*　　*

Woodthorpe Hall was sold by Sir John de Rhodes in 1599 to Bess of Hardwick who used the materials from this partially demolished mansion in the rebuilding of Bolsover Castle. Sir John was said to be a dissipated person who had been married three times. His second wife died as a result of the ill-usage she suffered at his hands shortly after the birth of their blind son whom the father later disinherited. The ghosts of the mother and her blind child were said to have been frequently seen in the vicinity of the ruined hall.

Sir George Reresby Sitwell wrote of his home, Renishaw Hall, that "of family history, absolutely nothing had come down to us but the tradition that our ancestors had lived there since the reign of Elizabeth, and a story concerning a portrait of the 'Boy in red' (his name forgotten), who had died by drowning, and whose ghost was supposed to haunt the house".

Peakland Poltergeists and Paranormal Puzzles

WHEN I have been speaking at various meetings on the subject of Derbyshire ghost stories, or during private interviews with individuals, a number of inexplicable stories have been volunteered from time to time. Some of these have been quite incredible and yet they have been certified with the utmost sincerity and sobriety by people of impeccable honesty and integrity. These particular stories, some not actually concerned with phantom phenomena, often verge upon the supernatural and pose problems for which I am—as an admittedly very unprofessional researcher—at a loss to find rational or satisfactory answers.

Some of the happenings appear to have been due to the performance of poltergeists; members of a mysterious and mischievous race belonging to the spirit realms which have an unpleasant habit of creating considerable disturbance in the physical sphere without any cause or provocation. Other stories seem to suggest paranormal pressures and influences brought to bear upon human circumstances in such a way that spiritual forces are invoked to interfere with material objects. Articles in cabinets have been disarranged; a system of domestic bells set ringing without human activation; a clock on one solitary occasion struck an irregular hour; another always stops at the hour its owner died; an electric bulb was mysteriously detached from its socket and fell to the ground without injury to the filament; a picture of a horse was removed in the night and found uninjured at the opposite side of the room; a sewing-machine was temporarily immobilised; a duplicate key appeared on a doorstep without explanation, and paintings were removed from the walls of a billiards room.

How can such things happen? What is the secret of the invisible powers that can so easily set at defiance the natural laws by which we and our world are governed? Forensic examination of the affected items would reveal no finger prints on them, for they have been displaced or disarranged by unseen agencies. But, without entering further into any questions or inconclusive arguments which may only confuse the issue (and myself at the same time), I will record the happenings without any attempt at exposition or explanation.

It was at Edale W.I. that Mrs. Tym told the meeting of an experience which occurred when her mother was bed-ridden by an illness from which there was no prospect of recovery. Crêpe-de-chine was a fashionable material for female clothing at the time and the invalid expressed the wish to have a crêpe-de-chine blouse, although there was little likelihood that she would ever wear it. Her daughter, who was an expert needlewoman, decided to satisfy this whim and set to work on her return home the same night with patterns, material and sewing-machine to produce the required garment. At one particular stage in assembling the blouse, the foot of the machine jammed and, although she tried the use of lubricants and resorted to other expedients to release the mechanism, Mrs. Tym had to admit failure and decided to resume the attempt the next day. But, the following morning, the postman brought news of her mother's death which had occurred at the precise time the machine had so stubbornly refused its services. Out of curiosity, Mrs. Tym went to her machine, turned the handle and it performed its normal function without a hitch!

*   *   *

Among several ghostly incidents related by Mr. F. A. Radford, concerning his residence at Bleaklow Farm on Longstone Edge, was an experience which happened one Saturday night when he and his brother were absorbed in watching a thrilling episode of the Late Night Movie programme on television. Suddenly there was a loud crash and the startled brothers found that the clock, which normally stood on top of a china cabinet, had fallen over and all the articles on the shelves were thrown into violent disarray. It seemed as though some invisible hand had swept over every item on display, silencing the clock in the process. Somewhat shaken by the experience the two brothers switched off the television set and retired to bed with a minimum of delay. The following morning, to their amazement, instead of finding the confusion they had witnessed the previous night, they found the clock ticking cheerfully away in its accustomed upright position, while all the objects in the cabinet had been restored to their usual ordered ranks. Nor could they find any trace of cracks, chips or breakages which would have appeared to be inevitable in such circumstances.

*   *   *

Chesterfield has a story of an old-fashioned house known as "Rose Hill" which was situated near the present Town Hall, and in which the bell system was subject to the caprice of some unseen campanologist. There are many well authenticated stories of the bells ringing even after the pull wires had been severed or immediately after being released from the restraining grasp of investigators. Correspondence concerning the supernatural ringing of these bells prompted a correspondent in the 1898 issue of **Notes and Queries** to supply the following anecdote:

"One who was with a well-known Derbyshire family, many years ago, remembers vividly at this time the scare that was occasioned by the uncanny behaviour of the house bells. A son of the house was at that time serving with the English in the Indian Mutiny. One evening, when the ladies had passed down to dinner, the bells in connection with the rooms were violently rung. The maids rushed in alarm to answer the summons, thinking it somewhat unusual to be called at that time of day. To their astonishment they found the chambers untenanted, and were thrown into a state of consternation through the strange occurrence. This unaccountable ringing at that particular hour was persisted in for some time; in fact, it is said until the arrival of the news of the soldier son's death. It was then remarked by one present that 'this is the meaning of the strange ringing of the bells'."

At a meeting of Chesterfield Townswomen's Guild, the President related a further instance of how inanimate objects can be subject to some form of spirit control. On this occasion it was one of those fascinating grandfather clocks which, not satisfied with supplying normal horological information, provides details of the current phases of the moon and days of the year. One night, while members of the family were preoccupied with a game of cards, the clock chimed twelve at exactly 9.30 p.m. This irregularity was noted by all present and prompted speculation as to the reason for this departure from accustomed routine. Concluding that it may have been due to some mechanical defect, particular note was taken of its subsequent striking performance, but this continued according to the regular pattern. Information was received about three weeks later that a close relative in Australia had died that particular night at exactly 9.30 p.m. (British time).

Mrs. Ollerenshaw, who lives in a cottage in Eyam Square, never allows her clock to run down if at all possible. For it always stops at 9.30 p.m., the time at which her husband died. She has also seen what may be the spectre of a former occupant of her cottage; an elderly lady in black dress and snow-white apron, the edge of which she was holding to her eye as though to wipe away a furtive tear during some moment of emotional stress.

* * *

At a Birchover W.I. meeting, the Secretary told a singular story about her then 18 years old cousin who lived in the village and whose hobby is collecting glass animals and birds. These she keeps in a cabinet for display. Two years previously she had been given an attractive glass swan which, when put on display in the cabinet, persistently refused to remain in its appointed position and was always found reversed as though shy at being observed. In the same house was the unhung picture of a horse which had defied every attempt to suspend it on the wall. It was always found undamaged, lying against the foot of the **opposite** wall to which it had been attached, with its cord unbroken and the glass intact.

Only the previous year the following incident had happened. The lady of the house had been papering a bedroom situated on the left side of the stairs, the treads of the latter being illuminated by a light at the top. She was standing on the step-ladder attaching the paper to the wall when something struck her in the middle of the back. Turning round she was astonished to find that the cause of the blow was an electric light bulb which lay innocently on the floor without having been broken. She was further surprised to discover that it was the bulb from a socket at the top of the stairs, and was perplexed as to how it had defied the law of gravity to swerve into the room instead of tumbling directly down the stairs. Moreover, when the bulb was replaced in the socket, she found that the delicate filament was undamaged and the bulb continued its usual supply of light.

Mention of Birchover reminds me of an incident concerning this village which was related by a vice-president of Holymoorside W.I. after I had given a talk on Derbyshire ghost stories. As a girl this lady had stayed with a friend at Birchover in a house which had formerly served as an inn. During the night she and her companion were awakened by a light being carried along the passage outside the room they occupied. The previous night, the young brother of her friend had been suffering from an attack of neuralgia, and the two girls concluded that he had perhaps been kept awake and gone downstairs to obtain an aspirin for relief. They called out to enquire if he was all right, but received no answer. Next morning they inquired into the circumstances of the boy's assumed quest for a sedative, only to discover that neither he nor any other member of the household had been abroad during the night. Nor could they find any explanation for the mysterious light moving along the passage.

*   *   *

An acquaintance of mine was employed on a local estate as chauffeur-gardener and later as estate agent. He told me of a strange experience which apparently foreshadowed a dramatic change in the fortunes of the family with whom he was in service. Discretion, it will be understood, dictates the withholding of names and locations. My informant has a family of two sons who

at that particular time were both suffering from German measles.
Parents and children were sleeping in the same bedroom because
of this illness. Shortly after retiring to bed one night, both
parents sat up simultaneously to watch a strange phenomenon.
A framed shaving mirror, standing on a set of drawers and leaning against the wall, slowly assumed a vertical position and
performed a gentle somersault before sliding down the front of
the drawers, resting momentarily upon each projecting knob
before slipping unbroken to the floor. This remarkable performance was watched with fascination by both husband and wife,
nor could they find any feasible explanation for the mirror's
strange behaviour.

The next morning my informant was invited by his employer
into the billiards room of the Hall where, to his astonishment,
he saw that every picture had fallen from the walls and lay
undamaged on the floor. Examination revealed that the support-
ing cords—and in some cases, wires—had been mysteriously
severed. The master, a retired military officer, refused to accept
any hint or suggestion that it was some ill-omen presaging trouble
or disaster; but shortly afterwards the family suffered a severe
reverse in fortune, involving the reluctant dismissal of several
members of the domestic staff.

*   *   *

An extraordinary incident was related by Mrs. H. Lomas, a
former officer of the now defunct Litton Women's Institute.
Whether it was a paranormal happening, or some strange coincidence, the reader may perhaps be able to decide. Mrs. Lomas
herself could offer no explanation, in spite of the fact that she
and her late husband, both prominent church workers, had
examined every angle and aspect of the mystery. In their home
is a piece of furniture which is a family heirloom; an old oak
bureau which has stood there for many years. It is unlocked with
a key which has the elaborate ornamentation typical of those
used for such furniture. One winter's day Mrs. Lomas found the
key to the bureau (as she supposed) lying beneath melting snow
on the threshold of their home. Picking it up she found that it
was rusted by exposure to the weather and concluded that it
must have accidentally fallen from the tablecloth when it had
been shaken at the door. But, when she went to insert the key
in the lock, she was astounded to find the usual key in its normal
position. Yet the newly found key was an exact replica; an
identical twin! Relatives and friends were subsequently inter-
rogated as to whether they had any knowledge of the duplicate
key, but the mystery has never been solved.

*   *   *

Then there was the strange story vouched for by Mr. and Mrs.
Dennis Slater concerning an incident which happened when they

were living in a cottage at East Bank, Winster. Occasionally they were awakened in the night by a series of spine-chilling bumps on the treads of the stairs—always the same number of bumps and always at the same intervals. One night Mr. Slater ventured downstairs to investigate the reason for the mysterious bumps. He hunted cautiously round the house, but nothing untoward was to be found except that the dog was cowering in a corner, its coat bristling with fear.

"Are you all right, Dennis?" called his wife anxiously, "is there anything wrong?"

"No!" was the reply, "not as far as I can see. Everything looks to be in order." Some while later, Mr. Slater tripped and fell downstairs. The same number of bumps! The same regularity! And never again were the Slaters troubled in their home by "things that go bump in the night". Mr. Slater had laid the ghost.

*   *   *

Another preternatural occurrence was related by Mrs. Hodges of Ilkeston, during a programme of ghost stories broadcast on Christmas Eve, 1972. It concerned a mystery announcement made by the B.B.C. (or apparently so) when interrupting a normal programme at 10.30 one morning to report a terrible earthquake tragedy which had devastated a certain town, the name of which began with "A", but which Mrs. Hodges could not remember at the time. She mentioned the happening to two of her neighbours who were hanging out washing, but who had not heard the announcement, and suggested that they would hear confirmation on the one o'clock news. She also mentioned the matter to her husband on his return from work. This was on February 28th, 1960.

But the day passed without any reference being made to the disaster on either the one o'clock or subsequent news programmes. Both Mr. Hodges and the two neighbours concluded that Mrs. Hodges had made some mistake or imagined the "news flash", and she went to bed that night a very perplexed and puzzled woman. The next day, however, the radio announcer broke into the morning programme at 10.30 to announce that preliminary reports were being received of a terrible earthquake at Agadir, a town on the Atlantic coast of southern Morocco. The announcement was phrased exactly as Mrs. Hodges had heard it on her radio the day before!

*   *   *

A lady whom I know very well as possessing psychic tendencies and clairvoyant gifts, and whom I respect for her honesty and personal integrity, told me of an occasion one Christmas when her family was young and they were having a party. Knowing her reputation for telling "fortunes" and the future from playing cards, the children prevailed upon her to give a demonstration of her skill. She acceded rather reluctantly to their request and a pack of cards was produced to provide the medium for telling the future. She interpreted the predictions concerning three of her sons without difficulty, but showed some hesitancy and momentary concern when reading the card of the eldest. However, recovering her composure, she continued to forecast his future. One of the cards selected indicated that the particular boy to whom it referred would take up a nautical career, even though he lived in so insular a county as Derbyshire; but, with the passing of years the prediction proved correct, for he did make the Royal Navy his chosen profession.

After the card session had ended, the father asked his wife the reason for her hesitation before making the final prediction and she replied with some apprehension that the card had been a complete blank, and she had fabricated a false forecast on the spur of the moment. During the following summer, when visiting a nearby village, the boys had been playing by the side of the River Derwent when the youngest fell into the water. The eldest boy plunged into the river and succeeded in rescuing his brother, but was himself unable to reach the bank and was swept away by the current. The mother and father told me the story of the blank card on the day of the funeral.

*   *   *

Many years ago the large store which supplied our village and district with anything from cattle food to candles and paraffin to postage stamps had been broken into during the night and burgled, but the police were unable to trace the thieves. The proprietor had reason to suspect certain residents in the village, but could offer no proof to establish their guilt. For his own satisfaction, however, he visited a noted Nottingham medium who was the "seventh child of a seventh child" and therefore renowned for the possession of supersensory powers. After the storekeeper had described the circumstances of the theft, the medium retired for a while and then returned to relate exactly how the crime had been committed. The homeward route from the scene of the burglary was minutely described, the thieves having crossed a disused mine-hillock, then a small field, entered the churchyard by a step-stile—where they rested the stolen property—and then resumed their journey to a cottage just west of the church and to which they descended by several steps. It was the cottage of the suspected thief and his accomplices.

Although this account fully confirmed the suspicions of the storekeeper, it could not be offered or accepted as evidence in a court of law, and the guilt of the thieves was never established other than by the seventh child of a seventh child. But the iron bars inserted in the windows to protect the property from similar violation in the future can still be seen.

*   *   *

Some phantoms seem to have preserved an attachment for articles of furniture for which they must have had a particular affection during their physical lifetime. And what more likely than a comfortable armchair? A luxury in which we may relax by the fireside; in which the book or newspaper falls upon our lap as we doze and drift into dreams of other days and dimensions of time.

After I had spoken at Coal Aston W.I., one member of the audience stated that her brother had a modern suite of offices built upon the site of the former Norton aerodrome. The upper part of the premises is reached by a dual stairway linked with a landing. On the landing stood a venerable chair, moth-eaten and showing other evidence of age. Ascending this stairway one day, the speaker declared that she was not a little surprised to see an elderly gentleman occupying the chair, yet, upon closer inspection, the chair was vacant. She was so convinced by the reality of the presence that she enquired of her brother whether their father was in the building—but the answer was in the negative.

Another lady at the same meeting stated that her sister had become possessed of a secondhand chair and, it transpired, of its former occupant. The chair was described as being of the folding type and very comfortable. One day, turning from her ironing-board, the sister was startled to see a soldier, complete with puttees and Great War uniform, reclining in the chair. This was the first of several occasions on which the chair was seen to be occupied by the same person. The family later moved house and felt that the soldier would be left behind during the flitting operation. But not so. For they soon found that he had settled in with them in their new environment and was again seen ensconced in his favourite chair. The housewife thereupon performed her own act of exorcism by disposing of the haunted chair—and they never saw the soldier again.

49

HOW can phantoms produce such sounds as sighing, sobbing, singing or speech when they have neither lungs, vocal chords, nor any of the physical organs essential to respiration and articulation? How, too, can they create such reflected sounds as footsteps, bumps on stair treads, beating of hooves, or splashing of water, when they have no physical weight to cause an impact? These are some of the thoughts and questions which filter through my mind as I write about supernatural songs and singers.

Ebenezer Rhodes, in his **Peak Scenery,** tells of a haunted oratory at Tideswell. He says: "The most interesting specimen of antiquity which Tideswell possessed was a stone chapel or oratory, which stood on the left of the road, on the entrance into the town from Middleton. This structure was apparently much older than the church, and it was probably erected before the reign of King John; but its antiquity could not preserve it from being taken down and sold to the best bidder. When it was unfloored and dug up at the time of its demolition, many human bones were found within it. Two large Gothic windows, of two compartments each, occupied the ends of this building, one of which looked upon the road, and the other faced the eminence called The Cliff. These windows were formed by three equal pilasters, which were surmounted with heads, one male and two female, that were sculptured in stone; and a pointed Gothic arch, rising from two slightly ornamented buttresses, composed the porch or entrance into this old structure.

"Such a place in such a country, must necessarily have something supernatural attached to it: it was accordingly peopled, by village superstition, with the visionary beings of another world. From this place, so long as it existed, unseen choristers were sometimes distinctly heard hymning the sweetest strains, as they seemed to pass in slow procession along the vaulted passages of the chapel to the chancel of the church, where the sounds gradually died away. This ceremony, whenever it happened, indicated the approaching death of some of the more important personages in the place, and no gospel truth was ever more religiously believed than was the occasional occurrence of these supernatural sounds. Persons whose veracity on other occasions could not be doubted, have solemnly averred the pretended fact."

Why Rhodes should have the temerity to so pompously discountenance this long established tradition is a puzzle to me. I am quite prepared to accept such testimony, even though I have no personal proof of its veracity; but lack of direct evidence does not give me authority to attempt to discredit the statements made by honest and sincere people. I have never set foot on the continent of Australia, but I believe the witness of those who have as to the existence of such a country, and surely such a principle of toleration ought to apply in the relationship between persons who have psychic perception and those who, like myself, have not.

In her **Vignettes of Derbyshire,** Mary Sterndale also describes the architecture of this ancient building at Tideswell which, after being desecrated to secular uses, was occupied by her sister, and she records that "against the death of any of the family there were always heard voices singing psalms in the ancient tongue; that the voices passed through the archway, and continued singing very sweetly till they reached the church porch, when the sounds died away; affirming she herself heard them a few days before her husband's death, Mr. Allen Middleton, who died in 1746; also that a picture of one of the Allens always slided from its frame previous to the death of any one of the family".

*   *   *

I was told that occupants of a house at Alderwasley hear the sound of singing proceeding from the empty and disused private chapel of the Hurt family. At the same house footsteps are heard shuffling along the stone chippings on a footpath leading to the door. These are terminated by a knock on the door, but when it is answered there is no one standing on the step. A door-bell was installed at the house and since then the unseen caller has adopted this means of summoning the occupants to the door! But I would think that such a village ought to be haunted, for it has a field called Killcroft and a farm with the lugubrious name of Buryhill Farm—place-names which must have been born out of some sinister circumstances in the past.

It may be recalled that in his account of the rising of spirits at Hayfield Church in 1745, the Rev. Dr. James Clegg reported that they "ascended directly towards Heaven, singing in Consert all along as they mounted thro' the Air . . ."

*   *   *

After I had spoken to a TWG group meeting at Belper on the ghost story theme, a lady from the audience related a brief story concerning a friend who lived at Kirk Hallam and whose home was haunted by a little choirboy. The chorister sang with charming sweetness and sometimes shared his landlady's bed, for she could not only feel an occasional irritating nudge from her

51

ghostly companion, but in the morning always found a dent in the pillow where his head had lain! My informant had been out of touch with her friend for some time, but made an agreement that if I would promise to speak to a Derby social group in which she was interested, then she would obtain more details in the meantime. At the time of writing, I am still awaiting developments along these lines.

*　　*　　*

The following report concerned a Matlock lady who was descended from the Ashford poet, John Howe, and it was attested by her son who was a man of probity and religious conviction. He wrote: "My mother had intelligence above the average of her class; she could in a moment give a piece of poetry upon any subject that was being discussed: it seemed to come like a flash of inspiration. I do not mean that she composed the verses, but that she seemed to have a library of poetry stored up in her memory which she could call up at will.

"My mother, after the death of my father, lived with myself and family in a cottage at Matlock. Almost a year before she passed away, she used to say in the morning: 'Did any of you hear music and singing about three or four o'clock this morning?' We all said 'No!' (Our room adjoined hers, only divided by a single brick wall.) We thought it was fancy on her part, and she said that she heard singing in the night two and sometimes three days in the week. At first she described it as distant music, but in a few weeks she could distinguish the words sung, and sometimes she knew the tune. At last she heard the music every time she awoke in the night or when she lay passive.

"A little niece about thirteen years of age at times slept with her, and she woke her up and said to her, 'Can you hear the singing? It is so plain.' She listened, but heard nothing. At last she was quite sure the singing was supernatural, and often described it as music from a full choir of singers, and she became so attached to it that she seemed quite disappointed when she missed it. She often told us about the singing, and sometimes could tell us the music and the words; often the words of a hymn, but at times secular music. I well remember one evening, about 11 p.m., as I sat in the house alone, all the rest of the family being in bed, my mother (who had been in her room some time), seeing a light downstairs, came down, and she said to me, 'Come, is it not time to go to bed?' Then she suddenly said, 'Now cannot you hear them singing?' I could not.

"My son, to whom I mentioned the circumstance, wrote: 'It seems like reflex action of the brain; the phonograph of memory —giving over again the musical tones with which the person was most in sympathy, and which consequently cut the deepest

Tideswell church, the "Cathedral of the Peak", to which choristers were heard chanting in Latin as they walked in procession by an underground passage from an ancient chapel. This was said to presage a death in the resident family (page 50).

Above:— A culvert at Derby in which a boy was asked what he was doing there, whereupon he replied "I live here" and vanished (page 40).

Opposite:— Top: Hazlebadge Hall, to which the returning ghost of Margaret Vernon rides furiously from Hope church on wild and stormy nights (page 23).

Bottom: The cottage at Curbar where a bespectacled old woman was seen "with her hair screwed into a bun and wearing a black poncho" (page 38).

Chesterfield's crooked spire, reputedly formed when Satan twisted his tail round the steeple (page 78). (From an old drawing showing the ancient hospital which stood near the church.)

grooves upon the cylinder of memory: a rehearsal of life's joys.' But at times she heard quite strange music that she knew nothing of and could only describe as beautiful. These supernatural songsters kept her company during wakeful nights, and continued with her to the last.

"A few years ago my only brother passed away. A week before his death his little daughter passed on, and I sat up with her the last night. I left at 6 a.m. to go to my work. About 8 a.m., all at once, one of my sons, then a lad of about twelve years, and others in the house, heard singing. It seemed to come from above where my little niece, two-and-a-half years old, lay dying. My brother (who passed away in the next room a week later) was asked whether he had heard singing. He answered 'Yes: I have heard it several times in the night, and just now I have heard it again.' My little niece passed away a few minutes after the singing was heard."

*　　*　　*

It was at Winster, not far from Matlock, where I heard the account of a spectral soprano singing in the bedroom of a haunted cottage in East Bank. The cottage was then occupied by Mr. and Mrs. Dennis Slater who told me of the incident. A friend had called to watch television with Mr. Slater and, during the programme, he enquired whether Mrs. Slater was rehearsing for some musical engagement—she is well-known in the district as a vocalist—declaring that he could hear her singing upstairs. Mr. Slater explained that his wife was out at the nearby Wesleyan Reform Chapel, but the visitor persisted that he could hear her singing in the room above. To satisfy his own curiosity, Mr. Slater went to the foot of the stairs and was not a little bewildered to hear someone singing in a clear, soprano voice. He quickly ascended the stairs, but the mystery song had ceased and there was no trace of the singer. When he re-joined his guest, the latter was still convinced that he had heard Mrs. Slater singing, and what was still more strange was the fact that the man himself is quite deaf!

The Slaters, as related in the chapter on Peakland poltergeists, had another peculiar experience while living in the same cottage. In addition, the cottage was supposed to be haunted by a former occupant, a sailor who, having purchased the property, went off to sea and never returned: at least, not in the flesh. Often Mr. Slater heard footsteps crossing the bedroom floor, sometimes even as he lay in bed, and on one occasion his nephew saw the sailor in the bedroom, but prefers not to discuss the happening. Another relative ridiculed the idea until, one night, she was left in charge of the house while the Slaters were out. Upon their return they found all the lights still switched on, and the tele-

57

vision too, but the relative had hastily departed—having herself heard the phantom footsteps.

I would like to interject at this point that, when pursuing a line of enquiry during personal interviews, I try to be as clinical as a detective when interrogating a suspected criminal, or as a lawyer in the cross-examination of a witness. I have sometimes tried to extract a recantation, or engineer a contradiction during the statement of evidence or perhaps insert a subtle insinuation that the persons were deceived during some moment of mental confusion; but, though they have often agreed the incredulity of their statements, they have at the same time declined to make any retraction.

On one occasion when I was talking with Mr. Slater, I was accompanied by a friend who is as confirmed a sceptic as Ebenezer Rhodes concerning ghosts, and it was quite unnecessary to apply my usual techniques of cross-examination. My friend took the initiative and proposed a series of arguments in which he variously hinted that ghosts were but shadows created by subconscious suggestion; hoaxes played by the imagination; mental mirages, or dreams which invade the territory of wakefulness. But Mr. Slater's faith in what he **had seen** was unshaken by my friend's arguments about things **he had not seen,** and I mildly interposed the suggestion that Mr. Slater could provide an independent alibi on three occasions by quoting second witnesses who could corroborate his evidence.

The following incidents have no connection with the theme of supernatural music and melodies, but they were related to me by Mr. Slater. When a boy living at Birchover, he and his brother had a terrifying experience as they lay in bed one Sunday morning. A door opened in a blank papered wall, and a man of large stature entered the bedroom and stood resting his hands at the foot of the bed as he gazed at the fear-stricken occupants. After standing for what seemed an interminable length of time, the giant visitor left the room by the normal door, and in the blank wall through which he had entered there was no sign of crack or crevice in the wallpaper to identify the doorway through which he had passed!

Mr. Slater is admittedly psychic and has twice seen the ghost of a small old lady with a kind, gentle face, crossing the road at a bend below Winster Vicarage near the approach to what is now the cemetery. At least one other Winster resident has seen the same old lady at the same spot, and he avoids travelling this stretch of road if at all possible. Both spectators agree that she wears a bonnet and old-fashioned dress. Mr. Slater affirms that when he has seen this spectre she has remained visible so long as he can refrain from blinking, but the flutter of an eyelid will cause her immediate dissolution.

8. The Stuff that Dreams are made of

AMONG a large assortment of newspaper cuttings, I found a
page torn from a women's magazine. It had neither date,
name, nor reference by which it could be identified; except the
surname of the person who had contributed the article for which
it had obviously been saved. This was rather baldly stated as
"Mrs. Braithwaite". I am sure that Mrs. Braithwaite would have
no objection to my passing on her story, because it was related
with such sincerity and strength of conviction. It concerned a
dream the writer had experienced as far back as 1936, and had
etched itself vividly upon her memory because of the sequel
that followed. She was living in Derbyshire at the time of the
happening.

One bleak day in February, Mrs. Braithwaite was visited by a
neighbour with whom she was very friendly. This lady took her
into confidence by disclosing that her doctor had advised consult-
ing a specialist concerning the cause of an illness from which she
had been suffering some length of time. This action had been
taken and the specialist had warned that, although an operation
was possible, there was some doubt as to the success of its out-
come. She and her husband had discussed the matter and decided
against the operation, feeling that this course was to be preferred
in that it would allow them to be together for the time—however
short—which remained to the wife. That same night Mrs. Braithwaite dreamed that she was walking down a certain lane near her
home when she saw, in a hedge otherwise bleached of colour, a
blackthorn bush in full bloom. A voice directed her to pick a
spray of the blossom and take it to her friend, advising them to
proceed with the operation and giving an assurance that the
issue would be successful.

The following morning there had been a heavy fall of snow
and Mrs. Braithwaite was exercising her Airedale dogs down the
nearby lane. The attention of the dogs was attracted to something of interest in the hedge bottom which seemed to require
their closer inspection. As she waited while the dogs snuffled
about the hedge bottom, she was amazed to see a blackthorn on
which was a spray in full bloom. Picking the blossom she felt
instinctively guided to the home of her friend to whom she
related the story of her dream and subsequent discovery of the

spray which she left in her possession. That same evening, the
friend and her husband called to say that they had talked over
the strange happening and were now convinced that the wife
should proceed with the operation. Mrs. Braithwaite's husband
was frankly shocked that they should be thus influenced by a
dream or intuition and urged them to seek further medical
advice. But his arguments were overruled by the couple who were
fully persuaded that they were pursuing the right course. The
operation took place in Derby Royal Infirmary and the spray of
blackthorn stood in a vase on the patient's bedside locker. During
the days of a long and serious illness, the husband was repeatedly
assured, "I shall get well".

Little did the patient know that the specialist had warned that
chances of recovery were very slender, but she had complete
faith in the miracle of the blackthorn. Its petals grew limp and
listless and one by one fluttered down, shrivelled and stained
and lifeless; the twig was withered and dry. But the patient was
eventually discharged, taking with her the dead stick to be
treasured as a keepsake and emblem of her faith in the forecast
made in her friend's dream. She survived the operation for 31
years and lived to the age of 87 years.

*   *   *

After speaking at a W.I. group meeting at Overseal, the President related to me an experience which happened to an aunt of
hers who lived in Derbyshire. The night previous to travelling
by car into Wales, this lady dreamed that a relief map of this
country covered the wall of her bedroom. She was fascinated by
the clarity of details and and these were so vividly impressed
upon her mind that, during the actual journey next day, she
instructed her niece—who was driving the car—to pull into a
lay-by round the next corner. The niece was rather perplexed
and inclined to argue the wisdom and expediency of this course,
but, on her passenger's insistence, obediently brought the car to
a halt in the lay-by. At the same time she felt puzzled as to how
her aunt could have known of the existence of this particular
lay-by. A few moments later, a lorry came careering down the
hill out of control and crashed into another with fatal consequences. The two shocked occupants of the car then realised
that the dream had averted what would otherwise have been
involvement for them in this accident!

*   *   *

Castleton has a classic story concerning the murder in the
Winnats Pass of a young couple said to be named Allan and

Clara who were believed to be eloping to Peak Forest—the then "Gretna Green of the Peak". The story has all the ingredients of a modern thriller—tenderness and terror, mystery and murder, villainy and violence, romance and retribution. It happened about the year 1758, and, although the story has been claimed to be apocryphal, there appears to be sufficient evidence to prove its historical accuracy. It has been told and re-told by many different writers, and one clergyman was inspired to present his own particular version in melodramatic—and rather mediocre—verse.

From their appearance and manner of dress, it was assumed that the young couple belonged to families of birth and breeding, although no outside enquiries appear to have been made into the circumstances attending their deaths, nor were they officially identified by relatives. This heightened the mystery surrounding their sudden disappearance, but may possibly be explained by the fact that their respective families did not know of their intended destination. Mounted upon richly caparisoned horses, the two riders called at the Royal Oak Inn at Stoney Middleton for refreshment and to enquire the way to Peak Forest; a circumstance which led to the general assumption that they were on their way to the Chapel of Charles, King and Martyr, for the purpose of being secretly married. While at Stoney Middleton they were overheard discussing a dream experienced by the young woman and which she felt was a premonition of impending danger. In this dream she and Allan had been walking through a crag-strewn valley when they were met by Clara's younger brother who had died about twelve years before. After several attempts she managed to speak his name, whereupon he pointed a warning finger towards an opposite hill and, after sadly shaking his head, had vanished. Looking in the direction he had indicated, Clara became aware of several ruffianly fellows who approached them in a menacing manner, seizing both and hurrying them into a gloomy cavern where Allan was brutally murdered. They were then in the act of threatening her own life when, with a suffocating shriek, she awoke. Nor could she eradicate from her mind the impression of this hideous nightmare.

Resuming their journey, the couple next called at a Castleton inn where it was "bargain night" with the lead-miners who were receiving their pay and spending it with customary celebrations. Four of the men saw Allan removing the saddle-bags from the horses and conjectured that these contained a considerable sum of money. Deciding to ambush the travellers in the lonely Winnats Pass, the men conscripted a blacksmith returning from his work at Odin's Mine and compelled him to join in their conspiracy. Meanwhile, suspecting the motives of the miners, the landlord and his wife had tried to dissuade the travellers from continuing their journey, but they insisted upon pressing on to their destina-

The Winnats Pass, Castleton, where an eloping couple are said to have been murdered in fulfilment of a dream.

tion. Their way led through the gloomy valley of the Winnats with its wild crags of grey limestone, and here they were startled by the five men who sprang out of hiding and threatened them with death unless they surrendered their money. The recollection of her dream was so vivid that Clara exclaimed, "O Allan, my dream, my dream!"

They were hurried into a nearby barn and, after being robbed of their money and valuables, were violently put to death as the attackers attempted to conceal the crime of theft by the more terrible crime of murder. Allan is said to have died as the result of a brutal attack with a pick-axe, but the manner in which Clara met her death is not known. A thunderstorm added to the confusion and terror of the guilty men who, sobered by the realisation of the consequences of their crime, covered the bodies with straw before sharing the £200 found in the possession of the murdered couple. With the intention of burying their victims the men returned to the scene of the crime at midnight, but hurriedly retreated as they imagined hearing shrieks of terror proceeding from the barn.

The following night the men summoned up courage to repeat the venture but, as they neared the site "two steeds, each mounted by a spectre, with hair dabbled with gore, rushed past and entered the barn". Again they failed to complete their gruesome task. But the third night they mastered their fears, putting the bodies in two sacks and hurriedly interring them by the light of a lantern some little distance from the barn. The horses were found wandering aimlessly, still saddled and bridled, on the hills between Castleton and Peak Forest, and were taken to Chatsworth as waifs and placed in the custody of the Duke of Devonshire, as the tenant of the Duchy of Lancaster. Years afterwards, two skeletons were discovered by lead-miners removing earth to sink an engine-shaft in the Winnats Pass. They were identified as those of the eloping couple by the fact that one of the skulls had a certain front tooth missing; a circumstance which had been noted both by witnesses at Castleton and Stoney Middleton. The skeletons were buried in Castleton churchyard. Clara's saddle of red Morocco leather may still be seen at the shop attached to the Speedwell Cavern.

Castleton people had suspected the five miners of being guilty of the crime, and especially when they each showed signs of sudden and unexplained prosperity. One man bought horses with his share of the money, but they are said to have died in quick succession, and he was often heard to confess on his journeys, "I have always a beautiful lady with me. She rides on my horse". Shortly after the crime, a daughter of one of the miners attended church in a rich silken dress which excited the notice of the whole village, and it transpired that this was the garment which had been removed from the body of the murdered woman. Tradition says that, although the murderers were never punished by sentence of human justice, they were all recompensed by what was considered to be divine judgement and none ever prospered or enjoyed his ill-gotten gains. One of them, some years after the discovery of the two bodies, fell from a precipice in the Winnats and was instantly killed; another died—to the astonishment of those who witnessed the incident—when crushed by a stone which fell from a hill near the place of the crime. One committed suicide by hanging, while another lost his reason and died miserably after making several attempts to take his own life. The last one, after lingering for ten weeks on his death-bed, made a full confession, exposing his confederates and declaring that Clara was "the handsomest woman he ever saw". He died the same day.

 # The Odd Experience

THIS title can be read two ways. It may refer to people who have had just an isolated or single experience of the super-natural, and it may also refer to the fact that the particular happening has been "odd" in the sense that they have found it unusual and inexplicable. Such people have not sought the experience and they have been unable to suggest an explanation as to why they should have been especially favoured. Such people are not ghost-hunters, psychic researchers or spiritualists, but just ordinary people who have made momentary and memorable contact with the spirit world.

I have read of phantom footprints appearing in newly fallen snow, but an even more intriguing story concerns an avenue near Hardwick Hall, and I have been assured that the following inci-dent happened one autumn day when a man and his dog were walking along the road which was littered ankle-deep with drifts of decaying leaves. The day was still, except for the crisp sound of leaves as they gently fluttered to the ground and lay unruffled by any breath of wind. Suddenly the dog began to behave in a strange manner, recoiling as though from some invisible source of danger and cringing with obvious fright. Its coat bristled with fear. Then the owner of the dog saw that the carpet of leaves was being stirred by invisible feet walking along the road, each step causing a fresh disturbance as the unseen pedestrian pro-ceeded along his way. And every effort to coax the dog to continue along the haunted road was in vain.

* * *

Mr. Brian Hickinson, of Hathersage, told me of an occasion when his mother, accompanied by a friend, was walking along the Hathersage-Bamford road. Upon reaching a point known as Sicklehome Hollow, the friend was terrified by the appearance of a white horse which was invisible to Mrs. Hickinson; a fact which naturally provoked an argument as to the existence or non-existence of the animal. One was positive that there was a horse, while the other was equally convinced to the contrary. In her excitement the friend grasped Mrs. Hickinson by the arm to point out the actual position of the animal, whereupon, at her touch, the latter was instantly made aware of the phantom horse. The two women left the scene without further argument, and without further delay.

Dr. Addy tells of instances of persons being made aware of phantom figures by the touch of companions who had the "sight".

*　　　*　　　*

Photographs of phantoms are exceedingly rare and even those which claim to be genuine are regarded with suspicion by sceptics because the camera is an instrument which can be deliberately manipulated to falsify facts. Nevertheless there seem to have been occasions when plates or films appear to have been sensitive to spirit impressions and images have been recorded which were invisible to the naked eye. A typical example is that of the Brown Lady of Raynham, in Norfolk, whose ethereal shape was photographed descending the haunted staircase.

In Derbyshire we have the record of an alleged spectre photographed by accident in Magpie Mine. Mr. R. A. H. O'Neil wrote that "just after the war (second world war) a party of speleologists were exploring the mine when one of them reported that he had seen a man with a candle walking along a tunnel from which he had disappeared without any trace. A photograph of another member of the party on a raft in a sough at the mine showed a second man standing, apparently, on nine feet of water . . ."

I was told of another instance at Bakewell when a social function was taking place. It was a garden party at the St. Anselm's School and one of the masters took a photograph of a group of visitors standing on some steps in the garden. When the picture was developed, it was seen that another figure—a boy in Victorian dress—had attached himself to the group. No one could identify the stranger from the past.

Thinking of phantom photography recalls the fact that Thursaston Hall in Cheshire was haunted by an old lady who was in the habit of pulling a bell-pull. She appeared so frequently to an artist who was staying at the house that he was able to make sketches of her features and produce a portrait of this visitor from the past!

*　　　*　　　*

In the December issue of **The Derbyshire Countryside** for 1956, Miss Sybil Young told of the following experience: "I first heard of her nearly twenty years ago. Shortly after I came to live at the cottage an old man from the village asked if I were not afraid of the ghost, and said that quite a number of people would not come up the valley after dark. I asked, 'What ghost?' and was told the story of a young girl who had drowned herself in my culvert after an unhappy love affair.

"Not however until the summer before last, on a hot afternoon in full sunlight, did I see her. My friend Joan was staying with

65

me and we spent one afternoon gardening. After a rest in deck
chairs with tea and small talk we decided to attack the weeds
in the rockery by the stream, and had worked there for over an
hour when Joan said she would stop and go to see her aunt, who
was ill. She went into the cottage and I continued the losing
battle. A short time later I paused to rest my back and saw Joan
by one of the deck chairs, leaning slightly over it. She was in her
underslip, and I called, 'Hey there, has the cottage demoralised
you?', as she was not the type of girl to wander round the garden
in her underwear! As soon as I had spoken I realised it was not
Joan, as her hair is short and this girl's hung in heavy loops over
each shoulder and framed her cheeks. I looked up at the bath-
room window and saw that Joan was there washing, and then
knew in an instant who my garden visitor was.

"When I turned to the chair again she had moved and was
just entering a little copse we call the Gypsy Dell—it leads to
the culvert. I got up quickly and ran to the opening, but when I
reached it she had disappeared. I was not frightened at all and
in my mind's eye I can see the girl now in the white dress, that
I thought was an underslip, with a dark belt, and the 'bangs' of
hair against her face. Strangely I cannot remember anything
below her knees although I am sure she was standing, and I
cannot remember her walking although she moved. I am so glad
I saw her and hope she comes back because she had been as
happy there as I am. Come again, little friend."

*   *   *

In another article in the same magazine, for the first quarter
of 1955, Miss Geraldine Mellor wrote: "My own experience of
the occult happened when, as a child, I lived in the north part of
Buxton, and one afternoon I went to look at a large empty house
near ours. After peering through the grimy windows into a
succession of big gloomy rooms, I was making my way out to the
road, when I happened to look round and into the window of a
small outhouse which was empty when I passed a moment before.
Now, however, I witnessed an extremely eerie happening. A
pair of dead white hands with long tapering fingers suddenly
materialised before me, and proceeded to fold a newspaper into
four—and the hands were not attached to a body!"

*   *   *

Stories of supernatural scents are by no means uncommon and
I wonder sometimes whether some of these could be induced by
an association of ideas. This suggestion was reinforced when I
was chatting with Mrs. H. Land, of Bonsall, and when she
recalled an incident concerning her father who had been a
carpenter by trade. Two points were made clear during the con-

66

versation. The father had carved some of the furniture (including the pulpit) at Imperial Road Methodist Church at Matlock, and during his lifetime, when suffering from colds, he had always resorted to a medical preparation called Famel Syrup as a remedy. Some years after the father's death, Mrs. Land, her sister and other members of the family were attending a service at Imperial Road (now closed as a place of worship) and were sitting near to the pulpit. Suddenly both Mrs. Land and her sister became conscious of a strong aroma of Famel Syrup. Yet other members of the family—whose sense of smell was by no means impaired— were sitting with them, but were totally unaware of this particular smell.

I have written elsewhere about a daughter who had a sudden intuition that her deceased mother was present in spirit with her in the room where she was sitting. The impression of nearness was so strong that she felt as if, by simply stretching out her arm, she could have touched her. Instinctively she exclaimed "Mother!" and immediately her nostrils were assailed by the smell of a combination of eucalyptus oil and Dettol, which deodorants had been used for sanitary purposes upon the occasion of her mother's death and towards which the daughter had subsequently developed feelings of revulsion and nausea. In both these instances the smell of well-known medical preparations had been simulated.

But some smells cannot be explained by any such principle as the association of ideas. I was told of a house in Glossop where occasionally there is an unaccountable smell of burning bread, even though no actual baking is in progress. It has been noted by the occupants that smells particularly occur when the wife returns home after an absence; but never when the husband has been away. One wonders whether a former mistress of the house had a King Alfred experience, or whether she left some bread baking and, by some mischance, never returned to remove it from the oven. At Earl Sterndale, I heard of a house haunted by the pleasant and appetising smell of newly baked bread, and the occupants construe this as an indication that their home has a history of happiness and contentment. Which makes me even more puzzled by this perfumery from the past.

*   *   *

Mr. L. Atkins, a devout churchman of New Whittington, undoubtedly has the gift of "second sight" and can tell many stories of psychic and supernatural significance in which he has been personally involved in his long life. On one occasion he was informed by the landlady of a certain hotel that she frequently saw a hand reflected in a certain mirror as though it were beckoning to claim her attention. When she turned

67

round, however, there was never a visible hand to match the reflection. This experience had persisted for some time, and Mr. Atkins advised that the owner of the hand was anxious to impart some information to the lady whereupon she decided to approach the brewery company for permission to remove the mirror to investigate whether anything at the rear was causing the mysterious reflection. A representative of the company replied to the effect that they were not only willing to grant permission, but would undertake the work to help satisfy the landlady's curiosity and allay her concern. When the mirror was removed from its position on the wall, a recess or cupboard was found in which there was a box containing a large sum of money and a will dictating the terms of its disposal. Further investigation revealed that three beneficiaries from the will were still alive and able to enjoy their inheritance. And the mirror lost its magic —the owner of the hand was satisfied!

*   *   *

Mrs. D. Bullard is the seventh child of a seventh child and has had experiences which confirm that this genealogical coincidence does qualify a person in possessing powers of supersensory perception. One evening, as a girl living in the village of Elton, she was returning home from running an errand when she encountered a white hen. The bird was fluttering about in her path, so she attempted gently to brush it away with her foot when, to her surprise, there was no physical resistance and her foot passed through the feathered phantom. This was concluded to be an ill-omen and her father died shortly afterwards.

*   *   *

While working at Sallet Hole Mine, near Stoney Middleton, Mr. Bernard Marshall believes that he saw a spectre of "th' owd mon". This collective name is applied to previous generations of lead-miners who worked the metalliferous veins which fissure the limestone to a considerable depth. Bernard was working in the "Unwin Vein" with a foreman electrician who is reluctant to confirm or deny the happening, but who admits that there was certainly "someone or something". But Bernard declares that the figure was wearing a long check coat and a flat cap, and that it simply vanished from sight. Few modern miners would be wearing such clothing and mine regulations insist upon the wearing of a safety helmet, not a hat or cloth cap.

Other miners have encountered these spectres which seem to be condemned to eternal wanderings in the underground galleries where corroded iron tools, fragments of rotting leather, old wagons and clay pipes are occasionally found to recall the activities of this former race of miners. At Hanging Flatt Mine,

68

"th' owd mon" has been heard shuffling along the workings muttering to himself, and has been seen with a spade over his shoulder both underground and on surface. One lady distinctly heard the muffled strokes of his pick, even though the mine was closed and securely locked at the time.

*   *   *

Mr. W. D. Goodall, of Matlock, told me of an experience when he saw his mother two years after her death. He was on leave from the Forces at the time and, due to the fact that his cousin Valerie was staying at his home, he was sharing a bedroom with his father. During the night he became aware of a figure in the bedroom and, knowing the mischievous nature of "Val", immediately concluded that she was up to her tricks and playing a prank at his expense. Crossing the room quietly to give the girl a surprise by switching on the light, he was the one to be surprised when he recognised the form of his mother standing in the sudden glow of light. In a few seconds she vanished.

*   *   *

The Alvaston story of thundering hooves recalls another Commonwealth echo of the sinister clashing of swords in a bedroom of the picturesquely gabled Hall at Youlgreave. This room is known as the Duel Room because a Cavalier and Roundhead are said to have fought a duel to the death there one November night during the Civil War. And on the anniversary of this bygone struggle, the two combatants thrust and parry with phantom steel as they re-enact an otherwise forgotten bit of history. One wonders whether a lady of divided loyalties might have been involved, or whether the disputants were just defending their less romantic political beliefs.

Mrs. H. Johnson, of Winster, told me that her father—a gamekeeper—used to describe how he had been compelled to press close against a wall as a coach and eight horses thundered past him at Roughwood Hollow between Youlgreave and Middleton-by-Youlgreave. He felt a strong draught as the horses and vehicle went sweeping past. Someone told me that the coach was sometimes illuminated by lamps; another person spoke of a coach and horses being seen on the same road near Hawley's Bridge, and that it was accompanied by running dogs.

*   *   *

The father of a young Grindleford business man told me of his son's experience when driving his Austin Seven car from Eyam to Grindleford. He returned home shaken and upset, and his parents elicited that on the journey he had seen an indistinct figure, shrouded in cloak and hood, cross the road from the top

69

of Jacob's Ladder, an old bridle-road climbing steeply from Stoney Middleton. He had stopped his car and watched the figure pass through the solid stone wall to proceed up the old cart-track in the direction of the disused Riley slate-pits. Shocked and dazed by the experience, he sat at the wheel some time before recovering sufficient composure to resume his journey home. The father, who is a man of sterling integrity, and with an opinion not easily swayed by prejudice, vouched for the truth of the statement, and the latter's shrewdness in business proved him to be a practical and matter-of-fact person who had no room for deceit or melodramatic exaggeration of the truth.

Now what he saw would correspond with my own idea of a spectre: an insubstantial spirit image wreathed in a shroud-like astral attire; the same impalpable and formless wraith which seems to be the embodiment of most artist's conception of a ghost. Yet many ghosts have the appearance of physical solidity and are clothed in garments which have a realistic quality; textures which, apparently, one could handle, as instanced by the man in the blue pin-stripe suit at Castleton, or the rector's wife at Glossop in her brown dress and head scarf, or the top-hatted and frock-coated gentleman at Over Haddon, or the headless woman at Dore with her green satin dress trimmed with coffee-coloured lace. But perhaps costumes and clothing—which are identical with those worn by the phantoms during the days of their mortality—are just as essential as the carts and coaches in which they rode, or the pair of crutches which supported the old shopkeeper as she hobbled up to the shop she used to keep in Alvaston. And a rather alarming thought. If swords clashing as their owners thrust and parry, or the sound of a pistol discharged, can be heard, is it possible these weapons might have a lethal effect upon the present generation?

I have also read of phantom fires, the warmth of which could be felt by the human spectator, and of a phantom house with illuminated windows; and in each case when the beholders returned the next day to the scene of their experience, they could find neither the ashes of the fire, nor a stone of the vanished house. I can perhaps understand the reflected shadow or image of a human being, a horse, or a dog being restored to temporary visibility. They have lived and breathed, possessed emotions and instincts, and therefore had a spiritual as well as bodily existence. But not so with carts, coaches and crutches; they are altogether soul-less and inanimate, although we notice that in all cases there is an affinity or an attachment between them and some phantom human or animal. They are an integral part of an impermanent scene, completing, as it were, the setting in which the spirits re-enact their drama to a small but privileged audience of humans who have the gift of "second sight".

Such mysteries as these are beyond my powers of reasoning
and rationalisation, and I am tempted to conclude that spirits
have a transitory existence (of varying time duration) until they
have adjusted to the circumstances and conditions of the continuing life. Some of them do not appear to have escaped the
physical defects and infirmities with which they were afflicted
in mortal life, as in the case of the Alvaston shopkeeper who
still depended upon her crutches, and the blind son of Sir John
de Rhodes who had not recovered his sight, or the little old
lady at Curbar who still needed her steel-rimmed spectacles. As
I think of limping and lameness, groaning and asthmatical
wheezing, I am led to ponder whether the blind are still deprived
of sight, and the sick do not find a cure or the lame a buoyant
step until they have come to terms with the continuing life?

Occult Occurrences in Ordinary Houses

WHEN pursuing my amateur researches into the science of the supernatural, I was at first inclined to cultivate the impression that stately homes should have a particular claim to phantom phenomena, yet, rather to the contrary, I have found that some ordinary houses have acquired a much more positive reputation for being haunted than some of the mansions in which the pattern of history has been shaped. Some council tenements and terraced houses have been given more prominence and publicity by the activities of ghostly residents who have seemed anxious to integrate with present-day occupants than have the ancient and historic homes of ducal families in Derbyshire.

Ghosts are often difficult enough to recognise—particularly the headless variety—but when they attach themselves to modern residences in which no deaths or sensational happenings have taken place, then it makes identification even more impossible. One explanation is that the sites were possibly occupied in past days by properties which have long since been demolished, and the modern intrusion is accidental in that the ghost may be re-living an experience which belongs to a different dimension in time. Here again, such metaphysical mysteries are beyond my comprehension. If there is an answer, it totally eludes (or deludes) me.

In a modern council house at Grimsby, tenants were troubled by the persistent perfume of embalming spices during the year 1959. Twenty people testified to having experienced the smell and also to having seen doors opening in the house. Researchers, including two clergymen, confirmed that the house was definitely haunted and five people stated that they had seen a ghost there. The evidence was so convincing that the Council agreed to the transfer of the tenants to another house on the estate.

*   *   *

Pleasley is on the Derbyshire-Nottinghamshire border. Early in 1965 a railwayman and his family in this village solicited the help of the rector, the Rev. A. Doncaster, and the Assistant Bishop of Derby, the Rt. Rev. T. Parfitt, to try and rid their home of ghostly tenants and a poltergeist. They also enlisted the help of the local Rural District Council to find them alternative accommodation. Mr. and Mrs. Frederick Slater lived at Midland Cottages and they testified to having seen ghosts and also suffering damage due to the obvious activities of a poltergeist. Crockery was broken; photographs damaged; a savings book torn up and statuettes of saints displaced in a cabinet. The first ghost was seen by their son, David, who was ill in bed at the time and who was startled to wakefulness by the fact that a grey-haired old woman was sitting in a rocking-chair beside his bed. She had a shawl round her shoulders, wore spectacles and was busily engaged in knitting some garment. The terrified boy plunged his head beneath the bedclothes until he felt that he was alone once more.

David's mother twice saw a tall figure in the bedroom which she described as "wearing a white robe and gliding round the room to leave through a closed door". Mr. Slater saw a person standing near the fireplace weeping. She was old and wrinkled, about five feet three inches tall and dressed in white, and also had white hair. When Mr. Slater asked the plaintive figure the reason for her distress, she made no reply but continued quietly weeping as though her grief was inconsolable.

*   *   *

Screened on three sides by sheltering trees, Bleaklow is a lonely and rather cheerless looking farmhouse built on the spine of Longstone Edge, but having the compensation of a lovely panoramic view towards the south. It reminds me of some exile nursing bitter memories of a sad and melancholy past. Nearby are some ancient entrenchments where a prehistoric battle is said to have been fought, and in one of the plantations is a barrow which was opened in 1848 and found to contain two primitive vases made of earthenware and deposits of human and animal remains. In one corner of the rock-hewn sepulchre lay the "decayed skeleton of a child of tender years". The syllable "low" in many place-names denotes the existence of a prehistoric burial-place, and the once exposed site of this grave earned it the rather sinister name of "bleak low".

When an epidemic of typhus struck the nearby village of Great Longstone last century, Bleaklow was the only place where it proved fatal, two victims dying of the disease. It was also here that, many years ago, a farmer or gamekeeper was responsible for the murder of his housekeeper one Christmas Eve. In a violent temper he chased her from the house with a carving-knife and forced her into a pool of water among the spoil-heaps of the lead workings behind the farm, and there she was drowned. I remember, as a boy, an old and rather eccentric resident of Eyam taking me to see the exact place where the murder was committed. He had been, I believe, a juryman at the subsequent murder trial. Mr. F. A. Radford, who lived for some years at the

farm, told me that he had witnessed a re-enactment of the murder
one Christmas Eve, and claimed to have seen the terrified housekeeper being pursued by her murderer brandishing a carving-
knife, to vanish at the site of the pool. On another occasion he
had also seen figures approaching along the rough road in the
light of his car headlamps and they too disappeared as he drew
nearer to them.

The departure of visitors from the farm was usually a sign for
supernatural activities to begin and there would be much opening and closing of doors, together with the incidence of icy
draughts. One night, when two friends and their children were
spending the night at Bleaklow, the parents saw a shadowy figure
cross the bedroom floor to bend over the sleeping children. They
were so terrified that they kept the light on for the remainder
of the night. Mr. Radford had heard of some vague connection
between a child and the farm, and said that the family had often
heard pitiful cries in the darkness outside. Subsequent searches
seemed to locate the plaintive voice among the nearby trees, but
no human source could be found. One is tempted to wonder
whether it might have been the spirit of the child "of tender
years" buried in the ancient tumulus among the wind-swept
trees, or whether it was that of one of the victims of the typhus
epidemic.

*   *   *

South Head Farm, situated between Edale and Hayfield, was
a mid-17th century house which has long been demolished.
According to tradition, a murder was committed at this lonely
farm upwards of three centuries ago. The daughter of the house
was killed in her bedroom by a jealous suitor who suspected her
of unfaithfulness. After committing the foul deed, the murderer
dragged her body downstairs and across a field to dispose of it
in a stream where it might be assumed that she had died by
accident or suicide.

Members of the Bradbury family, who were the last tenants
to occupy the farm, often heard a series of muffled bumps on
the stairs, as though a corpse was being dragged down them.
The meadow between the farm and stream was said to be haunted
by a girl in white, and this tradition was startlingly confirmed
by three Irishmen during the early days of this century. They
were casual labourers employed during the hay harvest and had
no knowledge of the supposed hauntings. Along with the farmer
and his sons, they were making hay in the haunted meadow,
when one of them inquired, "Who's the girl running down to the
stream?" The Bradburys were surprised at the question, for they
could see no sign of a girl, whereupon the Irishman ran to the

place where he claimed to have seen her running, but the wraith had vanished from his sight.

*   *   *

Edale is a village which has its own anthology of ghost stories. Residents have heard a phantom splash as though a body had been pitched into a pool where a pack-horse bridge spans the tiny River Noe. The splash is preceded by a prolonged and blood-curdling scream, and these sounds are said to be the echo of an incident when a boy was dragged from the now ruined Edale Head Farm to be drowned in the stream. Galloping horses have been heard at the crossroads near the village, and three parish councillors returning from a meeting distinctly heard such sounds. Under the impression that the horses were runaways, the three men took their stand in the road to try and arrest the animals. Although the moon was shining brightly, the astonished men were unable to see the oncoming horses and stood helpless and amazed as the sound of beating hooves galloped past them and died away in the distance.

*   *   *

The well-known record of the ringing bells at Rosehill, Chesterfield, was forcibly brought to my mind by a story I heard at Shipley (near Heanor) when I was invited to judge a competition for the best ghost story written and related by W.I. members. The most impressive story concerned the experience of one member and this happened when she was a young woman living with her parents at Derby. She had gone to the trouble of illustrating her story with a detailed plan of the house in which the incident happened, and further explained that owing to the distance between the living quarters and the front door, a battery bell had been installed so that callers could be more conveniently heard.

On this particular occasion, the speaker's father and a relative had gone to visit her sick mother in hospital, and she had been left in charge of the house in which a decorator was at work in one of the rooms. Some while after her father's departure, the door bell rang and was answered by the daughter who found no one at the door. A little later the incident was repeated and again investigation revealed no caller. Suspecting that the decorator was perhaps playing a hoax on her (although she admitted that he was a quiet, middle-aged man who was carrying out his duties with due diligence and attention), the young woman accused the man of playing a prank at her expense. But the charge was indignantly refuted and his denial accepted. So the young woman stationed herself near the door to await any recurrence of the mysterious happening.

75

Nor did she have to wait long, for again the bell rang vigorously and was promptly answered. Yet again there was no visible evidence of the cause and the bell began to ring with frightening insistence. With the help of the decorator the young woman disconnected the wires leading to the battery, but the bell continued to ring without the normally necessary power. Eventually it was reduced to silence; but on the father's return from hospital he broke the sad news that his wife would not recover from her illness.

11. Some of Derbyshire's Satan Stories

WHEN employed as a valet to a resident of Eyam, Mr. Percy Parkin told me of an experience he had during his former employment at Silver Hill Colliery, not far from Hardwick Hall. He was cycling to work with a fellow collier one day, when the latter made the unnerving discovery that they had been joined by no less a person than Satan himself, also mounted on a cycle. He first drew attention to the fact by making the startling announcement, "The Devil's riding at my side!" At first, Mr. Parkin treated the continued references to the Devil as something of a joke and made what he thought were suitably facetious replies, but when his companion insisted that their fellow traveller was keeping pace—whether fast or slow, uphill or down—with them, he began to question his mental stability and felt not a little relieved when they reached their destination. But his friend's behaviour was still strange. He had developed such a conviction of impending danger that he refused to collect his lamp and enter the cage to descend the pit. Instead, he remounted his cycle and returned home. And the man who took his place was killed at the coal-face!

This story reminds us that Derbyshire has several legends concerning the Prince of Darkness. At Chrome Hill we hear of the Devil's Parlour where he is said to have made an unsuccessful attempt to commit suicide. At Coxbench we find an earthwork known as the Devil's Shovel Full. An old record says: "In the valley between the castle hill and the hamlet is a large circular mound of considerable elevation by the brook, obviously a barrow or tumulus. The old people call it 'The Devil's Shovel Full'. They relate that his Satanic Majesty, when at Chesterfield, for some cause or other, resolved to dam the Derwent at Derby, and for this purpose was making his way through Coxbench with an enormous shovel full of earth. Unfortunately, however, he lost his shoe, and was compelled to deposit his burden in the valley."

Investigating this legend, Mr. R. W. P. Cockerton, of Bakewell, examined the site and concluded that it did not resemble a tumulus, and appeared too large to be of artificial origin. He suggested that it could be a glacial moraine, adding that "if it should prove on investigation to be of artificial origin, it must assuredly rank as one of the wonders of Derbyshire. Though one might be inclined to admit the powers possessed by his Satanic Majesty in the matter of damming, one would hesitate to suggest that the round 'shoes' discovered twelve feet below the clay so near to this spot had anything to do with this legendary event, even though the 'shoes' might have been suitable for use with a cloven hoof".

The Chesterfield legend tells of Satan making an aerial journey from Sheffield to Nottingham. Deciding to take a rest on the convenient steeple of Chesterfield church, he twisted his tail round the tip for greater security. His meditation was disturbed when a whiff of incense rose from the altar and assailed his unholy nostrils, whereupon he was so enraged as to resume his flight without taking the precaution of unwrapping his tail, causing the spire to assume its present-day deformity. A more attractive reason for its crippled appearance is that told when a young lady of peerless beauty was married at the church. As the bride approached, the steeple was so enraptured and bewitched by her beauty that it bowed in admiration and was never again able to resume its upright posture!

There is an old proverb which asserts that "Man proposes, but God disposes". But Duffield has a story which contradicts this claim, for it maintains that the eternal enemy of the Christian faith was responsible for choosing the site of the church in this village: "There is a singular tradition in this village regarding the removal of the Church from its intended site to that which it now occupies, by the arch fiend. At this village was anciently a castle belonging to the Ferrars, Earls of Derby. The site of this castle is still known by the name of Castle Orchards, and at a very short distance from the hill on which the castle stood is another eminence (only one field's breadth off), on which are some ancient cottages. There is a tradition current in the neighbourhood, that the church was originally intended to be built on this eminence, but after the work had been commenced and proceeded to some extent, the devil, for some unexplained reason, removed the whole of the work in one night to the site it now occupies, in a field by the side of the River Derwent, at quite the opposite end of the village. The workmen were naturally surprised in the morning at finding that their work had all disappeared, and after solemn prayer, again began laying the foundations, but to be carried away again by the devil on the succeeding night. Day after day the same thing was enacted, the whole of the material brought in the day being removed and set up in its right place on the site the arch-fiend had chosen for it; and at last he so completely triumphed over the patience of the workmen, that they went down to the place where he had

carried the material, and completed the church where it now
stands. The eminence, it appears, on which the church was
originally intended to be built, was a place of rendezvous for
evil spirits, for at the present day the villagers firmly believe a
'brown-man', or bogey, is to be seen every night near the
cottages."

Such stories are not altogether unusual. Sussex has two
churches which are said to have had their originally chosen sites
altered by supernatural interference. Legend says that the foundations of Alfriston Church, the "cathedral of the South Downs",
were first cut in a meadow called Savyne Croft. "There day after
day the builders laid their stones, arriving each following morning
to find them moved to the Tye, the field where the church now
stands. At last the meaning of the miracle entered their heads
and the church was erected on the new site." The other instance
was at Udimore where the church was first planned to stand on
the opposite side of the small River Ree. "The builders began
their work, but every night saw the removal of the stones to the
present site, while a mysterious voice uttered the words 'O'er
the mere! O'er the mere!' which not only confirmed the site of
the church but gave rise to the name Udimore."

Rather than thwarting the work of church construction and
frustrating the activities of religious builders, Derbyshire has an
instance of a chapel being built at the instigation of, and inform-
ally dedicated to, the Devil. This is the Halter Devil Chapel at
Hulland Ward, near Mugginton, which owes its existence to the
combined influence of the Prince of Darkness and one of his
reformed disciples. This chapel was founded in 1723 and endowed
with 18 acres of land by a certain farmer named Francis Brown,
although it has never been officially consecrated.

There are several stories as to how it originated, but the one
most generally accepted says that Farmer Brown "once had
occasion to make a journey after nightfall. The night was wild
and stormy, and vivid flashes of lightning, accompanied by
terrific peals of thunder, followed each other in quick succession.
A servant boy was sent to bring his horse out of the field, but
the boy, terrified by the thunder, was unable to catch the animal
and returned without it. Brown was a drunken, dissolute, devil-
may-care man, and, taking the halter from the boy, he swore
that if he couldn't halter the horse he would halter the Devil.
Lantern in hand he went to the field, secured what he thought
was his horse and brought it to the stable, where it vanished in
a flash of lightning. From that time Brown became a changed
man, and built a chapel and endowed it with 18 acres of land
on condition that divine service be held therein once a month
by the rector of Mugginton". Towards the end of the last century,
the chapel was rebuilt at a cost of £70, and previous to this

restoration there had been a stone over the doorway inscribed
with the couplet and date:

> "Francis Brown in his old age
> Did build him here an hermitage."

Some local wit painted the additional couplet:

> "Who being old and full of evil
> He one night haltered the devil."